Selected Letters of
General Thomas Woodward's
Reminiscences

Books by Nina Cooper

Servants on Horses
Published by Distinction Press

Translations by Nina Cooper

File No. 113 by Emile Gaboriau
Published by Distinction Press

The Ferry Mystery by Fortuné du Boisgobey
Published by Distinction Press

Monsieur Lecoq by Emile Gaboriau
Published by Black Coat Press

Coming from Distinction Press

The Omnibus Crime by Fortuné du Boisgobey

Also by Nina Cooper

The following work appeared in *Polyphony Magazine*,
April–June 2010:

LE PETIT VIEUX DES BATIGNOLLES
by Emile Gaboriau, translated by Nina Cooper.

"The Birth of the Detective Story"
CerisePress.com, Spring 2011, Vol. 2, Issue 6.

Selected Letters of General Thomas Woodward's Reminiscences

1857–1859

Regarding the Creek, or Muskogee, Indians of Alabama and Georgia

Edited by Nina Cooper

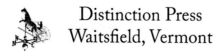

Distinction Press
Waitsfield, Vermont

Nina Cooper holds a Ph.D. in Romance Languages from the University of Texas at Austin. She has done critical work on the plays of Gabriel Marcel and Jean-Paul Sartre, as well as on the short stories of Julien Green.

Published by Distinction Press, LLC
354 Hastings Rd, Waitsfield, Vermont 05673
802-496-3271 • www.distinctionpress.com

Cover design and layout by Kitty Werner, RSBPress, LLC

Cover photo by Kitty Werner of James Earle Fraser's sculpture *The End of the Trail* is used with permission, courtesy of the Shelburne Museum, Shelburne, Vermont. The original bronze sculpture can be seen at the Webb Gallery at the museum. www.shelburnemuseum.org

Cover portrait of Yoholo Micco of the Creek town of Eufala. Head of the Tallassee Indians. Supplied by the Author.

ISBN: 978-0-9802175-6-8

Contents

Editor's Preface   vii

Biographical Sketch of General Woodward   xiii

J. J. Hooker Introduction — *Montgomery Mail* 1859   xxv

Representative Participants in the
Creek Indian Wars   xxix

The Letters

May 2, 1857   33

December 9, 1857   36

December 24, 1857   40

January 10, 1858   43

March 21, 1858   49

March 25, 1858   52

April 2, 1858   54

April 25, 1858   58

June 13, 1858   62

Letter of John Banks, From Columbus, Georgia *Sun*   65

June 16, 1858   67

June 21, 1858   72

July 8, 1858   79

August 12, 1858   87

September 16, 1858   89

October 20, 1858   91

October 31, 1858   98

November 3, 1858   114

November 25, 1858   116

Editor's Preface

The first forty years of the 19th Century were violent and decisive both for the Muskogees of the Southern States and for the United States as a whole. The Constitution of the United States had been adopted in 1787 and ratified by the last state in 1791. Many of its signers and supporters had serious reservations about some of its provisions. The Southern States, slave-holding and surrounded by the Muskogees, the Five Civilized Tribes, in Georgia, Alabama and the Carolinas and by the Seminoles in Florida held to their belief that the individual States possessed certain rights not specified by the Constitution, but reserved to the States and the people. The area had been colonized prior to the American Revolution by the Spanish in Florida and the English in the States near the Atlantic Ocean, extending inland to today's Louisiana.

During the earliest settlements, the large plantation owners interfered little with the Muskogees, who were not migratory as were the Indigenous Peoples of the Southwest. They were labeled "civilized" because they had permanent dwellings, organized leadership, laws, and smaller and larger tribes shared the same language with few differences. The larger tribes had initially absorbed smaller groups, which then took the name of the more populous tribe. For many years, men from England, Ireland, Scotland, and some few from France, had come to hunt and trap, few bringing wives and families. Many lived among the Muskogees, marrying their women, obeying their laws, and settling into their way of life. Since Muskogee law did not forbid polygamy, many had both white and Muskogee wives. Frequently, the half-breed family and the extended family of cousins, aunts, uncles, and grandparents coexisted with the all-white family.

As events in the upper States changed, small farmers with families, as well as single hunters and trappers moved further into the South. Conflicts arose among the various groups, each new group pushing the Muskogee further from traditional hunting grounds and forests. By the time the English prepared in 1812 to attempt to re-take the Colonies lost in the Revolutionary War, loyalties among Muskogee groups to either the Americans or the British had already been formed. Although the Creeks were a single cohesive group, the Americans had arbitrarily divided them into "Upper" and "Lower" Creeks, depending on which side of the Chattahoochee River they were located. Those on the east side, closer to Tennessee, Kentucky and the Carolinas, supported the Americans, since for many years they had been assimilated into white culture. Those on the west side supported the British.

After the War of 1812, the lands of both those who had supported the Americans and those who had supported the British were expropriated, ostensibly because Indian uprisings began with some murders along the Tennessee frontier, but also because the influx of white settlers created a need for more land than had already been ceded in treaties between the Americans and Indians. The Tennessee Militia, and later the American Army, under the leadership of General Andrew Jackson, began a campaign to annihilate the Creeks. The result was The Indian Wars which lasted until General Jackson became President Jackson and signed the Indian Removal Act in 1838, clearing the way for expansion of United States White citizens into Alabama and Georgia.

Thomas S. Woodward (1794?/1797?–1859), a mixed-breed Muskogee with a small amount of Muskogee blood, began his career in the army as a scout for General Jackson. He had lived among the Muskogees, knew their language, and had friends among both the Whites and the Creeks. Among the Indians he was called Chulatarla Emathla. He participated in the Indian Wars in Alabama and Georgia, and also in Florida, which had been ceded to the United States by Spain. He played a role there setting up a government and pursuing a war of annihilation against the Seminoles, who were pushed into the Everglades, but never surrendered.

After the Indian Removal Act, General Woodward moved from Alabama to Arkansas and then back to Louisiana. He continued to correspond with friends in Georgia and Alabama and to keep abreast of events by subscribing to newspapers there. He found that those contributing stories about the events which took place twenty years earlier had romanticized and distorted historical fact. He also found that the romanticized stories were told from the point of view of the Whites. He was principally concerned with correcting some second-hand accounts which he had read in the *History of Alabama*, by Colonel Albert James Pickett.

In 1857 he began trying to correct some of those stories by corresponding with the editor of the Montgomery, Alabama *Mail*. The editor, with his permission, published those letters in 1859, the year of Woodward's death. He had a remarkable memory and in his letters he shows himself both amused and ironic when he remembers his role in those events and does not attempt to apologize for his own life. He sets down his admiration for some of those on both sides of the conflicts, Creeks, mixed-breeds, and Whites.

In the letters to J. J. Hooper from the first letter to the letter dated November 27th, 1858, General Woodward speaks little about himself. He died the next month on December 24th. J. J. Hooper, his editor, places his last letters with others to him at the end of the letter of November 27th in an Appendix. Almost all these letters concern his early life and answer many questions the readers of the earlier letters must have had and which will perhaps not only interest the today's reader, but serve as a background to the men and times of the Muskogee Wars. The current editor has therefore placed his biographical information found in the letters in the Appendix as an introduction to the earlier letters.

After the Indian Removal Act, General Woodward, now a rich man holding about forty slaves, moved to Arkansas and then to Louisiana. He was an honest and fair historian, but as he himself would have admitted, just a man, after all, and as such bound by his time and place. His sympathies are, of course, ultimately with General Andrew Jackson.

EDITOR'S NOTE: One difficulty for the contemporary reader is the fact that during the period in which General Woodward was writing, there were many half-breeds as well as white men who lived among the Creeks and sometimes had several names, Indian or White, and even sometimes two names in each of at least two languages, as for example: "He had frequent skirmishes with the Indians, under the control of Chitto-Fanna-Chula, or old Snake Bone, but known to you and the whites generally as old Ne-he-mathla." Most of these duplicate names General Woodward explains. The names of some of the more important participants in the Indian Wars are given as a preface to the present edition. The word "Micco," which recurs frequently is the equivalent of "Chief," or "Head Man."

General Woodward's spelling and punctuation have been kept, except in the case of obvious typographical errors by the typesetter. Paragraphing has been added to aid the contemporary reader.

This adaptation relates to the Muskogee Indians and the Indian Wars. Therefore, much of historical importance and interest concerning the founding of Alabama cities and the contributions of several important men of the period has been omitted here.

This work is intended as a companion piece to *Servants on Horses*, published in November 2009 by Distinction Press. Contrary to *General Thomas Woodward's Reminiscences*, *Servants on Horses* is fiction, but faithfully reproduces historical documents of the period. The novel tells the story of the Muskogees from the point of view of a Creek Muskogee of the Wind Clan. Taken together, *General Woodward's Reminiscences* and *Servants on Horses*, will, hopefully, give a total picture of the period 1799 through 1838. The last date is that of the Indian Removal Act, the end of the Muskogee Nation in Alabama and Georgia.

Biographical Sketch of General Woodward Summarized From His Letters in the Appendix to His Recollections

One of General Woodward's last letters, December 13, 1858, written shortly before his death, begins: "Dear Sir: Your letter of the 27th of November last came to this office some days back, and I would have tried to answer it before this, but have been too feeble to do so; and I now fear that I shall be unable to do justice to your inquiries, or answer them satisfactorily." Nevertheless, he does so in some detail. He begins with the information that the exact date of his birth was never recorded. His father died in 1800, his mother, who had remarried after the death of his father, died in 1806. Although his father had left a will leaving his considerable property, in land and in slaves, to be kept together until Thomas Woodward reached the age of twenty-one, the will was never consulted. The brother died shortly after Woodward's father. The sister was taken in by their mother's sister and soon after taken to Milledgeville, Georgia, then the capital of Georgia. No provision was made for Thomas. He was left to roam free until one of his mother's brothers took him in and sent him to school to "one John Posey, who taught in the State House, then an unoccupied building." Since he was older and bigger than other students he left school as often as possible to roam the country with boys his own size and age.

His mother's relatives in that family treated him well and he remained there for eighteen months or two years. One of his cousins married Robert Rutherford. His uncle was preparing to send one of his sons to Athens, Georgia, to college. Woodward remembered that "A Dr. Brown was then at the head of that institution. Rutherford proposed sending Woodward also. A second uncle objected, saying "it would be money thrown away," and Woodward states that because of that: "I never saw the inside of a College but once, and that was but for a few minutes, as I only went in to help another boy carry out his trunk, which he was unable to carry himself."

The uncle who had opposed his being sent to school employed him for the next year to plow for him. At the end of that time, he asked for payment for his year's work. Woodward recounts: "But my uncle was by that, as he was by the school money—he thought it would be 'throwing it away,' and of course he never paid me one cent."

At that, Woodward thought he could live more cheaply among the Indians and says: "From then until the Creek Indians migrated to Arkansas, I never lost an opportunity to make myself acquainted with their character and history."

In 1811, the uncle with whom he had lived in Milledgeville, sent to his step-father and obtained four of the Negroes who had belonged to his father's estate. His uncle sold one and purchased a piece of land and had the others work the land to support Woodward and his sister.

In 1812 Woodward entered the army as a private in the war against Great Britain. In 1813 his sister married General James C. Watson, who had no information concerning the estate of his wife's and Woodward's father. Rutherford put Woodward's affairs into the hands of Woodward's brother-in-law, saying: "Take Tom's little matters into your hands, and pay what will be right; for he (alluding to me) will do nothing while the war lasts but follow the army."

He entered the army July 1, 1812, and served in East Florida with General Daniel Newman. He says: "I done but little and saw less; but if it was foot-racing, wrestling, swimming, and the like, I was among the foremost." In 1813 and in 1814 he served under General Floyd. When the army returned home, he stayed to take charge of Fort Hull. Later, he met a group of sailors in a tavern, got drunk, got into a fight was rendered unconscious and woke up in the sloop *Epervier*, as a sailor. A sail was seen, the *Epervier* put out to sea, but tacked and returned to Savannah. He had been only a few days on board when he requested permission to return to Camp Covington. Permission was refused, and when the Captain and First Lieutenant were absent he jumped into the river and swam ashore. He remained in the vicinity of Camp Covington until his brother-in-law, General Watson, could employ a lawyer for him. He and his lawyer returned to the *Epervier* and when the Captain asked why he had jumped ship, he told him: "I was drunk when I shipped, and that I had asked his permission to go on shore, and he had refused me the privilege, and that I wished to see my friends before I left—for it had already been understood that if peace was made with Great Britain, that the *Epervier* was to go up the Mediterranean with a fleet under Commodore Decatur." Two sheriffs came aboard, served a writ of habeas corpus and he was taken to jail until he could appear in court.

He managed to inform the authorities there that his brother-in-law was a Quarter Master at Camp Covington. He also mentioned that his uncle was John Howard of Milledgeville. He was allowed to visit his brother-in-law and, until his court date, was allowed to take living accommodations in the city. When brought before the court he was discharged. He stayed about Savannah for several weeks and then returned to Milledgeville, then to visit relatives in South Carolina, and returned to Georgia into the Creek Nation. After some six weeks there he returned to Alabama. He says: "I there fell in with one Angus Gilchrist, and he and myself went to Nachadoches, Texas; there we found Edward McLauchlin, the best Indian interpreter I ever heard, except Billy Hamby. From Nachadoches we went everywhere. It would take one of John's kind of books to hold all that happened that year."

Although General Woodward's letters are not clear about the sequence of events at this point, he is clear that after being discharged from the sloop *Epervier*, he returned to Milledgeville in 1815 and was there informed by his uncle that his father's will was at the courthouse in Saundersville. He not only recovered his father's will but had an explanation from his uncle as to his uncle's behavior. His uncle told him: "Tom, no doubt you do, and will think you have been neglected; and you have to some extent a cause to think so. I and your uncle Ben Howard (alluding to another brother of his), are the only ones who did not oppose his marrying your mother. And it will do no good now to know their objections, and therefore I will let that pass." Woodward informed his uncle that he had been told the objections from his uncles on the Woodward side of the family. The objections stemmed from the fact that in the earliest days of the settlement of South Carolina prior to the American Revolution, an European came to Beaufort, South Carolina, and took a wife from among the Indians. Because of the Indian blood of this ancestor, a Silvester, through his daughter, which ran in the Woodward blood, his Howard relatives disapproved of what they considered a mixed-blood marriage.

In November of that year he was back in Georgia, and was employed by General Clark and several others to go to St. Augustine to find and return some run-away slaves. In January 1817 he traveled to North Carolina and returned to Georgia in March, and again went to Florida to capture and return run-away slaves. The attempt to capture them was deemed too hazardous, and he says: "I spent pretty much of that summer in the settlements on the Alabama river, and among the Indians." He also made claims on certain sections of land.

On his return to Georgia, he was told there was trouble with the Seminoles in Florida and he offered his services. He says: "My opponents were Capt. Joseph H. Howard, with whom I had served in two expeditions, and was my Captain in both—and Capt. John D. Broadnax, a very efficient officer, who had distinguished himself in Gen. Floyd's fights. But it so turned out that I got more votes than both of them. Gov. Rabun declared that he was gratified at my success, and would issue a commission forthwith, that I should have the title, if nothing else."

The troops were not ordered out immediately and so he bought an interest with a man named John Jeter in a tavern, had an interest in a Faro-Bank with a second partner, and other interests he called "too tedious to mention." Both his partners broke him and he says "I had nothing left but a Major's commission to depend upon." The troops were finally ordered to Fort Hawkins. He was the oldest Major and as there was no officer senior to him, he took command of two Battalions of Infantry and two troops of Cavalry. Two senior officers soon appeared and he says, "There was little done except foot-racing, wrestling and drinking whisky, when we could get it. The troops never went more than forty miles beyond the line."

Somewhat later there was an encounter with Indians when several soldiers were sent to meet a provision wagon. Two men were killed; the head of one was cut off and the other was scalped. He says: "as soon as they brought in Lee without his head and Loftis scalped, we (the twenty-two men who had volunteered to go to Fort Gaines to protect the women and children there) crossed the river, went to Chehaw, on Kitchafoony Creek, got fourteen Indian warriors and left the next morning. When they reached the Fort they thought it had been captured by the hostile Indians, but found the flickering light they saw was that in a room with two men playing cards. He took command. He says: "I called up all hands, went to the magazine and took out some guns, and informed them that every man who did not take a gun and do duty, should leave the Fort." When he was relieved at Fort Gaines, he was ordered by General Jackson to Fort Scott with as many friendly Indians as he could recruit. He arrived with some five hundred Indians, under two half-breed chiefs, Kinard and Lovet, as well as ammunition. That was in March 1818.

They began building Fort Gladsden and Woodward and General Jackson had their first disagreement. He says: "And as the matter has been often talked of, and misrepresented by some, I will here give you the particulars of that affair, as there are those yet living who witnessed it." He states that one company was comprised mostly of some very young men from the first families around Nashville. They did little but ride along the trail on the march and stroll about in camp where they pleased. One day they decided to give a Georgia militia man, much bedraggled and dirty, a bath in the river against his will. There were seven high-ranking officers present. One of the young men said to General Jackson: "General, we have a notion to wash that man." The General said nothing, but smiled. Woodward recounts: "That made me mad. They dragged Gilbert nearly to the water's edge. I remarked to Gen. Glasscock that was one of his men, but Glasscock said nothing. I then spoke out loud, and remarked that he was a Georgian, and had claims on me. I then walked to where Gilbert was, pulled him away from them, and ordered him to go to his quarters. They then attempted to seize me. I tapped or pushed one of them over; and another I pushed into the water, where it was about knee deep." Woodward showed his side arms, which were under his hunting shirt, to the boys and the scuffle ended.

The young man who had begun the fight began a quarrel with Woodward, saying the General Jackson had seen it and had said nothing, and that it was none of his business, "and besides, he said, I had no command among the whites, and that I had better attend to my Indians." Woodward says: "I told him it mattered not where my command was; that when I saw such chaps as him out of their place, I would put them in it. I discovered that the General was mad, for I had not been very choice about words or insinuations. He rose to his feet and said he had seen as big men as I was thrown into the water. I remarked to him that he might, but that he had not men enough in his Life Guard to put me in, and if he liked he could try it."

A Major Twiggs suggested to Woodward that he had better go to his quarters. A Captain Bee spoke so as to be heard by everyone: "Woodward is right, and Georgians ought to love him."

Woodward continued, "As I walked off, Gen. Jackson cursed me for a damned long, Indian-looking son-of-a-bitch (I recollect his language well). As he made that speech, I turned and said to him that I had some of the blood, but neither boasted of, nor was ashamed of it. I went to my quarters, and either sent a note or got Capt. Brown to go to the General, (I now forget which) and say to him that I regretted having incurred his displeasure, and that if he had no further use for my services, I would quit his camp.

"The evening or the next morning he sent for me to go to his quarters. He said to me that I done right in preventing the volunteers from throwing the militiaman in the water, but said I was too self-willed, and did not observe a proper respect towards my superiors, and that he wished the matter to drop there, and wished me to remain. There the matter ended."

In Florida "a fool Yankee," burned and plundered a town, killing women, old men, children, and an Indian chief. Jackson ordered him to be returned to a military tribunal.

The process was finally completed with Woodward's help. Jackson then offered him a commission in the regular army. He declined. He says: "After I quit the army in 1818, I went to Washington city with some half-breed Indians. I visited the eastern shore of Maryland, went into Delaware, returned to Georgia, and to Alabama as far as below Montgomery." He returned to Georgia in 1819, started various enterprises, one he had discussed with General Jackson, as a possible partner. In 1820 he went back to Alabama, where he was married. He says nothing about his wife, not even her name.

He comments on the following years: "I remained in Alabama some twenty years; managed my pecuniary matters badly most of the time, was very poor, was sold out twice by the sheriff; always voted on the weak side; was not very popular, often spoke too quick and too freely; had a family that was interesting to me at least, consequently had often to submit to indignities or insults from a little short stock that under other circumstances I should have slapped a rod. In 1841, I moved to Arkansas and lived there twelve years. The climate proved fatal to all my family except my eldest son, and it has so preyed upon him and myself that we are nothing more than the wrecks of what once were men."

Woodward ends this letter with what he says is a description of "the true disposition and character of General Jackson." He writes:

From the rapid manner in which my health has declined of late, I think it probable they are the last I shall give you or any one else. I shall close this by giving you what I think was the true disposition and character of Gen. Jackson. If he was not the most sensible and best man that I have known, he was the greatest man, with a large portion of the American people whom I have had any thing to do with. His mind was stronger and better cultivated than many have thought it to be; a man of bitter prejudices and unforgiving disposition, and a true friend when he really proposed it. He could not be corrupted with money; strictly honest in all monied transactions, despised flattery, though he often had it heaped upon him by the quantity in his latter days. The only ones who could flatter him were those whom he looked upon as being so low they could have no motive, and those who stood so high as not to be suspected. He preferred having his own judgment respected more than that of the balance of the world. If he bet ten dollars on a horse race, he would pay a hundred rather than lose the ten, for with the loss of ten dollars, would go his judgment.

He would never, for a moment, suffer himself to think that those he placed in office would act dishonest—he being honest in money matters himself—and that was the cause of there being some defaulters in office during his administration. He would admit of no superior, and was jealous of those whom the people looked upon as his equals and was not at all times a judge of his true friends. There were thousands who appreciated him properly and admired him for his good qualities, but opposed some of his arbitrary measures, and some had not voted for him. These he looked upon as his enemies, and never missed an opportunity to deal them a blow under the fifth rib. His popularity, at one time, and for a long time, was almost irresistible. He would suffer it used in the support of a friend, regardless of everything, when silence on his part would have placed him in a more enviable attitude with the more reflecting and intelligent portions of mankind.

I will cite one instance among many to show how far he would go. It has been the custom, and is expected, that demagogues and politicians will use every means to carry their points in elections, but there has always been one rule observed among our army and naval officers, and it never should be violated: for they established the rule and take them according to number, they are and have been the most thorough gentlemen I have any knowledge of. That rule was never for one officer to speak disparagingly of another, unless it was well known that he had been guilty of a gross violation of duty, or something else that had rendered him an unfit associate for the balance. Gen. Harrison had been a Major General in the army and resigned. Gen. Jackson succeeded to the command which Gen. Harrison would have held had he continued in the service. Gen. Jackson did much. He achieved a victory that the history of wars seldom records. The American people thanked him, they rewarded him, placed him in the highest office known to civilized men. But not to their credit do I say they submitted to his iron will, and in some instances a gross violation of their rights. It is well known, in a country like ours, that in some instances too high an estimate has been placed on military fame. It has governed in some of the most important elections, and has resulted in but little good to the country.

In 1840 Gen. Harrison was a candidacy for the Presidency. His friends seized upon his military deeds, and other things, as had Gen. Jackson's friends done before. Instead of remaining quiet and letting the people arrange their own matters, Gen. Jackson departed so far from what I think should have been his proper course as to write a letter, giving the people, and particularly his own friends, to understand that he never had looked upon Gen. Harrison as a military man. This was objectionable, coming from the source it did.

The times, and circumstances at the times, some men have lived, have had much to do in building or pulling down their fortunes. It is quite likely that if Oliver

Cromwell had lived in England at any other time than that in which he did live, from the reign of Egbert down to Victoria he would have been looked upon as being what he really was—a base hypocrite—Clay, Webster, Calhoun and Gaston (if the latter had possessed more ambition) would have been great at any age of the world, and so would Gen. Jackson have been more than an ordinary man at any time. And had he been old enough, and placed at the head of any army in the Revolution, no doubt he would have distinguished himself, but never would have been rated higher than many engaged in that service, and perhaps not as high as Green, Wayne, Stark, Daniel Morgan, or Ethan Allen. And had there, by chance or otherwise, been any one who was placed higher in the scale of greatness than himself, I think it quite likely that he would have evinced, or have shown, to some extent, a kind of jealousy to Charles Lee or Horatio Gates. Those of the Revolution were a different people to most of those in Gen. Jackson's time. In the Revolution, men were willing to serve, and if by chance they were killed, it would answer for their friends to read and speak of their deeds of daring. But not so in Gen. Jackson's time. There were too many who chose to live and see their names puffed in the newspapers, whether they merited it or not. Gen. Jackson knew the people he lived amongst, and knew how to control them and did it.

The best evidence I can give of his being a great man is, that without money and friends, he raised himself from an obscure Irish boy to the head of this nation, and was the most popular man that ever was and perhaps ever will be in it again. I have not said Irish boy from any invidious motive, or to detract any thing from his true merit. For I think if his true origin were known, it would only add to his standing, and prove to the world that he descended from a race of the right blood to make great men. One thing can be said of a truth, that he made more little would-be great-men, the last twenty years of his life, than God has made truly great ones for the last two centuries. And if his ambition, at times, caused him to err, his love of country made him a good patriot; and the American people will cherish his memory, particularly those living in his time, while he sleeps quietly where the laudations of sycophantic and hypocritical friends and the reproaches of his enemies cannot interrupt his repose.

Yours truly,
T. S. Woodward

Introduction

By J. J. Hooper

Most of the letters which are contained in this little volume were written by Gen. Woodward, without any idea of their being presented to the public in this form. Indeed, the first two, addressed to his friend Mr. Hanrick, were not expected to be published, at all; but being casually shown to the writer of this introduction, he solicited and obtained them for insertion in the columns of *The Montgomery Mail*, believing that their contents would prove attractive to a large class of readers who feel much interest in all that concerns the early history of the State. Subsequently, Gen. Woodward was kind enough to contribute to the "Mail," (with which the undersigned is connected as senior editor), a number of letters containing much valuable matter relative to the history, customs, &c. of the Creek Confederacy of Indian tribes. About the same time, friends of his caused the publication, in the *Columbus Sun* and the *Union Springs Gazette*, of several letters written by Gen. W. to them. All these letters, replete as they were with incidents and descriptions of a most interesting character, found favor with the public; and the undersigned was frequently applied to for copies of them, which it was impossible to supply. This suggested to him the idea of publishing the whole in a form convenient both for preservation and reference. He therefore immediately wrote to Gen. Woodward asking his consent to his having the letters collectively published. It was with some difficulty that his consent was obtained, as Gen. Woodward alleged that his want of early education and the inaccuracy of his style unfitted him to appear before the public as a writer of historical sketches. He only yielded, at length, to the argument that he alone, perhaps, of all living men, possessed knowledge of the many interesting facts and traditions he had acquired during an intercourse of nearly half a century with the Indian tribes of the South-west. These facts are stated with the view of disarming the hypercritical, who might be disposed to be severe upon the homely but effective phraseology with which the General's interesting narrations are clothed.

It is more than twenty years since the writer first saw and knew Gen. Woodward. His personal acquaintance with him was but slight; yet he knew well his reputation in East Alabama, as a brave, rough, warm-hearted man, of fine intellectual endowments, a most sagacious judge of character, extensive knowledge of Creek Indian history, manners and character—with an indemonstrable will and a sturdy self-reliance, which spoke of itself in his tall, sinewy form and strongly-marked, expressive face. A discriminating observer, at that time, would have selected him out of a thousand, as the man most fertile in resources, most indomitable in the execution of his plans, and possessing in the highest degree the physical qualities most needed in the emergencies and hardships of a semi-Indian life. His exterior was rough, his manners military and at times abrupt, but those who knew him best were well aware that he had a heart large enough for any deed of real benevolence. The presuming or pretentious he mercilessly flayed with a biting sarcasm, of which he was master; and many anecdotes are told, illustrative of his powers of repartee. But to the weak and unprotected, he was and is invariably considerate and kind. In proof of this, it may be mentioned here, that when he learned thro' Col. Banks in Columbus, Ga., that Mrs. Dill (whom he and others rescued from the Indians in Florida in 1818) was still living at or near Fort Gaines, he immediately transmitted, thro' the writer of this, a sum of money to Col. Banks, for the relief of the old lady's necessities.

Few men have had better opportunities for studying the Indian character and investigating their customs, than Gen. Woodward. Very early in life, as appears from two autobiographical letters which were received as so late a day as to compel their insertion in the Appendix to this little volume, he was brought into contact with the Red Man; and, stirred by the Indian blood in his own veins, he studied his character and traditions lovingly and earnestly. His early appointment to the command of a body of friendly Indians, in time of war, proves that he was considered to know them and to have influence over them.

As to the consideration in which Gen. Woodward was held by his superiors, it is not improper to state that the writer of this has now in his possession an original letter from Gen. Jackson, speaking of Gen. W., as "a brave, intrepid and gallant soldier." It bears date, "Nashville, September 30, 1819."

In conclusion, the writer of this would remark, that he believes that the unpretending pages which follow contain a very great deal of matter of high historical value to the people of Alabama and Georgia. For that reason, he has taken the trouble to collect such of the Letters as had been published previously and to induce Gen. Woodward to write others. For the task of arranging, pruning, etc., he has had neither time nor health; but he trusts that even in their present crude form, they effect much good, in the correction of several popular errors and in familiarizing our people of the later history of those tribes that have recently departed our borders.

Montgomery, Ala., Jan. 15, 1859

J. J. HOOPER

Representative Participants in the Creek Indian Wars

General Andrew Jackson *aka* Jacksa *aka* Chula Harjo

General Thomas Woodward *aka* Chulatarla Emathla

General William McIntosh, Jr. *aka* Billy McIntosh *aka* Tustunnuggee *aka* White Warrior

Colonel James A. Pickett—author of *History of Alabama*

William Weatherford *aka* Billy Larney *aka* Hoponicafutsahia *aka* Red Eagle

Colonel Hawkins—early Indian Agent among the Creeks

Tecumseh *aka* Pouncing Big Cat—Shawnee leader who tried to unite all American Indian tribes

Peekaboo *aka* Elkswatawa (The Loud Voice) *aka* Pemsquatawah (Open Door) *aka* The Prophet—brother of Tecumseh

Menauway *aka* Ogillis—Indian leader at Horseshoe Bend Massacre

Ussa Yoholo, Micco of the Creek town of Eufala—Head of the Tallassee Indians

Oceola *aka* Black Drink *aka* Billy Powell—Seminole leader. Grandson of Peter McQueen's sister who married William Powell. (Oceola was the principal leader among the Seminoles. He was tricked into coming in to a council. Bearing a white flag, he was nevertheless captured by General Thomas Jesup and imprisoned in Charleston, South Carolina, in 1837. He died the next year.)

Jim Boy *aka* High-Head-Jim *aka* Tustennuggee Emathla—chief Indian leader at Burnt Corn fight

Josiah Francis *aka* Illes Harjo (or Hildis Hardjo)—Indian leader called the Prophet, hanged by General Jackson

Ne-he-mathla Micco—Indian leader hanged with Josiah Francis by General Jackson

Peter McQueen—a leader at Burnt Corn Fight, son of James McQueen, Scottish emigrant, head of Tallassee Indians

Davy Tate—Descendant of early immigrant to U.S., half-brother of William Weatherford

Sam Moniac *aka* Samuel Takker *aka* Hadjo Moniac — descendant of early immigrant to U.S. and Creek wife

Big Warrior—Speaker for the Upper Creeks; signed the Treaty of Fort Jackson, 1814, The Treaty of Flint River, 1818, and the Indian Springs Treaty, January 8, 1821, ceding Creek Territory to the United States.

Sehoy McPherson—mother of Davy Tate and Billy Weatherford

Yargee—son of Big Warrior, married all three of Peter McQueens' daughters

Opothle Yoholo—leader of Creek delegation to Washington 1831–1832

Daniel McDonald *aka* Daniel McGillivray—father of Bit Nose Billy McGillivray

Tom Carr—Irish trader, father of Paddy Carr, 19-year-old interpreter to Washington with Creek Delegation

Selected Letters of General Thomas Woodward
1857–1859
Regarding the Creek, or Muskogee, Indians
of Alabama and Georgia

Adapted From:

General Thomas Woodward's Reminiscences
1857–1859
of the Creek, or Muskogee Indians
Contained in Letters to Friends in
Georgia and Alabama
From His Residence in Louisiana

I

WHEELING, WINN PARISH, LA.
MAY 2, 1857
E. HANRICK, Esq.,

My Old Friend,

The Montgomery Mail comes occasionally directed to me at this office; and whether the paper is paid for or not, I am unable to say, although I requested a gentleman to do so, and he says the money was forwarded. If such is not the case, call on the Editor and pay what is due, and also pay for another year's subscription, and write to me at this office, and you shall have your money immediately. It is through the *Mail* I frequently hear you are living, which I hope will be the case many years to come.

My friend, how time and things have changed since first we met! I think it has been forty years, the last winter, since I first saw you at Granville, Pitt county, N.C., rolling tar barrels. And your city, Montgomery, about that time, or shortly after, was started, or begun, by Andrew Dexter, and now, I suppose, is one of the most desirable spots in the Southwest.

I knew the spot where Montgomery stands before any white man ever thought of locating there. When I look back on things as they were and what they are now, it makes me feel—as I am—old. You and I have lived in fast times, which our heads will show, my friend; so, let it rock on—we will only sleep the sounder when it comes to our time to rest.

I see also announced in the *Mail* the death of several old friends, among them Gen. Shackelford, whom I have known from my boyhood. I was with him in Florida in 1812, in an expedition against the Seminoles. There are but few of that detachment of Georgians now living—in fact, I know of none, unless it be Dr. Fort, of Macon, Ga., John H. Howard of Columbus, Ga., Col. R. Broadnax, of Ala., and myself. If there are any more of them, it is very few, and I have lost the hang of them; but should I live, I well be in Milledgeville, Ga., on the first day of July 1862, which will be fifty years from the time we started on that expedition. If you are then living in Montgomery, I will give you a call.

I also see that my old friend, Major Thomas M. Cowles, is no more. He was a good man—I knew him before he was a man. He was fit to live in any country that God may think proper to occupy with honest men. He belonged to my staff, and accompanied me to Fort Mitchell, with an escort under the command of Gen. Wm. Taylor, to conduct Gen. LaFayette to Montgomery. I shall never forget a visit that Major Cowles and myself paid to Billy Weatherford, the Quadroon, him about whom so much has been said, and so little known. We remained some days, and among our crowd were Zach. McGirth, Davy Tait, the half-brother to Weatherford, old Sam. Moniac, who, many years before, had accompanied Alex McGillivray to New York, in General Washington's time.

I have often thought that I would give you and friend Hooper, of the *Mail*, a little sketch of what I had learned from those men and others, in relation to Indian matters; but they are all dead, and what I have heard and know would, in many instances, contradict what has gone to the world as history, and I do not know that mankind would be better off, even if I could undeceive and give them what I know in relation to Indian history, and so I will let it pass.

But still, there is one thing I want, if it can be got hold of, and, if George Stiggins is living in your country, he has it. It is a manuscript given to me by the widow of Col. Hawkins. It is in the handwriting of Christian Limbo, who lived with Col. Hawkins many years. It was copied from Col. Hawkins' own manuscript, which was burned shortly after his death. I knew Col. Hawkins well. He knew more about Indians and Indian history, and early settlements and expeditions of the several European nations that undertook to settle colonies in the South and Southwest, than all the men that ever have or will make a scrape of a pen upon the subject. The loss of his papers is certainly a very great loss to those who would wish to know things as they really were, and not as they wished them. Stiggins, as you know, had some learning, and was a half breed of the Netchis tribe, tho' raised among the Creeks. He spoke of writing a history of the Creeks and other Southern tribes, and I loaned him my papers. I assume he has done by this time what he contemplated, and please see him and get my papers, if you can, and take care of them until you have a chance to send them to me. You will also find among the papers some in my hand-writing, that I intended for a Mr. Daniel K. Whitaker, of Charleston, S.C., who was concerned in a Southern literary journal.

Yours,

T. S. W.

II

WHEELING, WINN PARISH, LA.,
DECEMBER 9, 1857

E. HANRICK, Esq.

My Old Friend, —Your letter came to hand safe, after taking its time, as I have, in going through the world, quite leisurely. You will find five dollars enclosed: pay yourself, and hand the other two and a half to the editor of the *Mail*: say to him, that after he has worked that out, and he learns that I have worked out, he may continue to send his paper. I see my letter to you, of May last, in the *Mail*. The editor speaks in very flattering terms of my capability in giving sketches and making them accurate and interesting. I would be proud that I could do so, and prove to his readers that he was not mistaken. It is true, I have known Alabama a great while, and many of its earliest settlers—particularly Indians and Indian countrymen. And I would most willingly, if I thought any facts that have come within my knowledge, or circumstances related to me by others in whom I could place the most implicit reliance, would be interesting to the readers of the *Mail*, give them. But as I write no better than in my younger days, but much worse; and as anything I might write would to most persons be of little interest, I must now abandon it. Besides, you know my capacity for embellishment (the only thing that suits too many readers) is not such as would render my sketches very interesting to many. I have no doubt but that, if I could be with you, and many more old acquaintances that I left in Alabama, (and hope they still live) and could get around a lightwood fire, I could interest you—or, at least, spin over old times and bring many things to your recollection that you have forgotten. (I do not allude to old store accounts. Though you have lost many, I never heard of your forgetting one.)

I often wish myself back in Alabama, and have as often regretted leaving Tuskegee. I was the founder of Tuskegee. I selected the place for the county site, or place for the court house, in 1833. I built the first house on that ridge, though James Dent built the first house on the court house square, after the lots were laid off. The day I made the selection, there was a great ball-play with the Tusgegees, Chunnanugges, Chehaws, and Tallesees. A Col. Deas, a South Carolinian, was with me. Ned, those were good days, were they not? I can never recall them, nor many other things that were very cheering to me then. I wonder if my five cedar trees, that I planted at the McGarr place when I owned it, are living yet? Ned, I, in company with my family, old Aunt Betsy Kurnells, (or Connells,) Tuskeneha, and old John McQueen, dug up those cedars, when they were very small, from under a large cedar that shaded the birth-place of Ussa Yoholo, or Black Drink, who, after the murder of General Thompson, in Florida, was known to the world as Oceola. This man was the great grandson of James McQueen. You know his father—the little Englishman, Powell. His mother was Polly Copinger. The railroad from Montgomery to West Point runs within five feet, if not over the place where the cabin stood in which Billy Powell, or Ussa Yoholo, was born. The old cedar was destroyed by

Gen. McIver's negroes, when grading the road. It was in an old field, between the Nufaupba (what is now called Ufaupee), and a little creek that the Indians called Catsa Bogah, which mouths just below where the railroad crosses Nufaupba; and on the Montgomery side of Nufaupba, and on a plantation owned by a Mr. Vaughn, when I left the country, rests the remains of old James McQueen, a Scotchman, who died in 1811, aged—from what Col. Hawkins and many others said he was 128 years old. He informed Col. Hawkins that he was born in 1683, and came into the Creek nation in 1716, a deserter from an English vessel anchored at St. Augustine, East Florida, for striking a naval officer.

When I planted those cedars, I had a wife and three children. I thought, then to make at the foot of them a resting place. But more than twenty years have elapsed, and many changes have taken place with me and with those that were with me then, and I care but little now when or where I may be picked up. But still, I would be glad to know that the cedars were spared; for none who knew the hands of those that assisted me in planting them there, could think of molesting them—unless there should be one with a marring hand, like him that destroyed the old lettered beech at the old Federal crossing of the Persimmon creek, and the old Council Oak that once stood in front of Suckey Kurnells' or Connells' house, which you knew well. Yes, it was under that oak, where you and I have heard many a good yarn spun, both by our white as well as red friends—many of whom have long since gone to that world of which we read and talk so much, and so much dreaded by many (if not more), and which never can be known to living man. Yes, friend, it was under that oak—held as sacred by the Indians, and should have been as memorable among Alabamians....

You have often heard of our mutual friend, old Capt. William Walker, tell about him and myself, camping there with Cols. Hawkins, Barnett and McDonald, of the army and Gen. John Sevier, one of the heroes of King's Mountain.... On the side of the Indians there were Billy McIntosh, Big Warrior, Alex. Kurnells, and many others. Kurnells was the interpreter, wearing that Iroquois coat you have often seen in the possession of the big woman, his wife. On that occasion, Kurnells exhibited many Indian curiosities; among them was the buck's horn, resembling a man's hand, which you have seen in my possession since.

This is becoming tedious to you, no doubt, and I must stop. But you can excuse it, as I live alone and have so little to employ my time about, that my mind is often led to contemplate things that have passed and would have been forgotten, but for my lonely situation. It affords me some satisfaction to think and talk (when I meet an old friend) of old times; and after commencing to write, these old things would appear, and I felt bound to give them some attention.

III

WINN PARISH, LA.
DEC. 24, 1857

J. J. HOOPER, Esq.,

I wrote a letter to my old friend, E. Hanrick, of Montgomery, last May, in which I spoke of giving you some few sketches of Indians and their history. Why I alluded to these things, I had a short time before seen an extract in your paper taken, I think from a Mobile paper, making some inquiry about true meaning or the signification of Alabama. And from the article, I supposed the writer to think that the word Alabama was of Jewish origin, by giving the name of Esau's wife, who spelt her name Al-i-ba-ma, (if she could spell). Now whether she borrowed her name from Jedediah Morse, or he the name from her, it matters not, as both spell it alike. The word Alabama, and many other words among the Indians, as well as customs, have been seized upon by some to establish a fact that never existed: that is, to prove that the North American Indian descended from the Lost Tribes of Israel. Now it would be as easy to prove that such tribes never existed, and much easier to prove that they dwindled away among those Eastern nations that frequently held them in bondage, than to prove that anything found in the native Indian is characteristic of the Jew. I have traveled among a great many tribes, and circumcision is unknown to them; and besides, and Indian in his native state is proverbial for his honesty, and from the records handed to us as authentic, the great Author of all nature was put to much trouble to keep the Jews and the property of their neighbors in their proper places

I will return to my letter. I see it published in an October number of your paper, and shortly after its appearance, I received a letter from a Mr. J. D. Driesbach, of Baldwin Co., Ala, requesting me to give him what information I could of the persons whose names were mentioned in my letters to Mr. Hanrick, and any thing I knew of Indians and their history that I thought would be interesting; also informing me that he had seen in the possession of George Stiggins, which had been loaned to Col. Pickett when he wrote the *History of Alabama*: and whether interesting or not, I scribbled off some twenty or thirty pages and sent to him, and among other things I gave him what I understood to be the origin of Alabama, as we have it from the Indians....

One other circumstance that convinces me that the Creeks and Alabamas had become pretty much one people before they settled Alabama and Georgia, is that the tribes they incorporated into their nation after settling the Creek country never would come into the family arrangement, which arrangement I will try and explain to you. They were laid off in families—that is, Bears, Wolves, Panthers, Foxes and many others—also, what they termed the Wind Family, which was allowed more authority than any family in the nation. There was nothing in their laws to prevent blood cousins from marrying, but never to marry in the same family—thus, a man of the Bear family could marry a woman of the Fox family, or any other family he pleased and the children would be called

41

Fox. In all cases, the children took the mother's family name. Years ago, you could not find an Indian in the nation but could tell you his family. But whisky has destroyed many of their old customs as well as the Indians themselves.

There is too much of this to publish, even if it were worth publishing. Read it, show it to Col. Pickett, burn it and send me his *History of Alabama*.

Yours,

T. S. W.

IV

WINN PARISH, LA.
JAN. 10, 1858

TO J. J. HOOPER, Esq.:

I wrote to you some time back some sketches relative to the Creek Indians, which no doubt you found too long, too tedious, and too uninteresting to publish. In that I sent you I made mention of a family arrangement among the Creeks that differed from all other tribes that I know or have traveled among. The Creeks are laid off in families, viz: Bears, Tigers, Wolves, Foxes, Deers, and almost all the animals that were known to them. All these families had certain privileges, and every one of a family knew to what family he belonged and what privileged were allowed. There was also what they termed the Wind family, which was allowed more privileges than all the rest. For instance, when an offender escaped from justice, all the families were permitted to pursue a certain number of days and no more, except the Wind family, which had the right to pursue and arrest at any time—there was no limit to their privileges in bringing an offender to justice. There was nothing to prevent blood relations from marrying with each other, but a woman of the Bear family was at liberty to take a husband in any family except a Bear; so it was with all the other families, but none were permitted to marry in the same family; for instance, if a man of the Wolf family marry a woman of the Fox family, the children would all be Foxes.

Such has been the custom among the Creeks from the earliest history I have had of them, through their intercourse with the whites has changed many of their old habits and customs even since my time. In fact, I know a number of words in their languages and names of things and places that are not spoken or pronounced as they were when I first knew them. This has been occasioned by whites not being able to give the Indian pronunciation, and the Indians in many cases have conformed to that of the whites. A horse, for instance, is now called Chelocko by the whites who speak Indian, and by most of the Indians; but originally it was Echo Tlocko, signifying a Big Deer—Echo is a deer and Tlocko is something large. The first horses the Creeks ever saw were those of the Spaniards, and they called them big deer, as they resembled that animal more than any other they knew—this is their tradition, and I am satisfied that it is correct.

There is an Indian town above Montgomery, Coowersartda, that is called by the whites Coosada; also the town Thelawalla, where Soto (de Soto) fought the Creeks, it is called by the whites Cuwally, and many of the Indians raised of late years call it as the whites do, and do not know what its original name was, nor what its meaning is. Thela is an arrow or bullet, and Walla is to roll; the proper name is Rolling Bullet; and many other such alterations have been made that have come within my knowledge. Indians in almost every instance learn our language quicker than we learn theirs, particularly our pronunciation. An Indian, if he speaks our language at all almost invariably pronounces it as those do from whom he learns it. If he learns it from a white man that speaks it well, the Indian does the same; if he learns it from a negro he pronounces as the negro does. You may take the best educated European that lives, that does not speak our language; let both learn it; if the Indian does not learn so much, he will always speak what he does learn more distinctly than the European. This will no doubt be disputed by many, but I know it to be true from actual observation, and I do not pretend to account for why it is so, unless it is intended that at some time Americans shall all be Americans.

I believe I mentioned the name of James McQueen before. This man came amongst the Creeks as early as 1716 and lived among them until 1811. He was said to be, by those who knew him well, very intelligent, and had taken great pains to make himself acquainted with the history of the Creeks. From the early day in which he came among them, and they knowing at that time but little of the whites, their traditions were, no doubt, much more reliable than anything that can now be obtained from them. From what I have learned from this man, or from those who learned it from him, the Muscogees, or as they were originally known to the other tribes, Musquas, and all the little towns or bands that composed the Creek confederacy, was a Confederacy before they crossed to the east of the Mississippi river. From what I have been able to learn, Musqua, or Muscogee, signified Independent.

Besides, I knew a Capt. John S. Porter, formerly of the U.S. Army, who, some thirty years ago, with a few Creeks of the McIntosh party in Arkansas, visited California and went up the Pacific coast to the Columbia river, and returned by way of the Salt Lake, and on his return to Arkansas he wrote to me, giving an account of his travels. The writing covered some three or four sheets of paper; a great deal of it was very interesting. I do not now recollect whether I loaned it to George Stiggins, or a Mr. Whitaker, of Charleston, S. C. But I recollect among the many accounts of his travels, that on the head waters, or at least the waters of the Colorado of the West, he found a small remnant of the original Musqua. They spoke mostly a broken Spanish dialect, but still retained much of their old language and old family customs. They gave pretty much the same account of being driven from their old homes that I have learned from the Creeks.

These people informed Capt. Porter that their nation was once strong, and they had many languages; that they inhabited the country between the Rio del Norte and Mississippi river, or Owea Coafka, or river of cane. They also gave him the original Indian name of the Del Norte, but I forget it; but Owea Coafka is what the Creeks call the Mississippi river. They also stated to him that they lived near the Gulf, on what they called Owea Thlocko Marhe, signifying the largest water. They say they were driven off by the Echo Thlocko Marhe, or horsemen, or what the creeks in our language would call the big deer men. Echothlock is a big deer, as I stated before, and the proper name of the horse Echothlock; Ulgee means horseman. They also stated that long after they left their old homes, and horses had become plenty, that the Indian learned the use of them, and that a number of the little tribes that once lived on the rivers and Gulf had taken to the prairies. They also gave Capt. Porter an account of a long war with some tribes high up on the Rio del Norte, and that one of the most warlike tribes had gone east. They called them as the present Creeks do, Hopungieasaw, and what are now known to the whites as Pyankeshaws. I recollect two women that Tuskenea carried to the Creek nation, of the Pyankeshaws, as the whites called them, but the Creeks call them Hopungieasaw, or dancing Indians.

But you see that I differ with Col. Pickett as to the early settlement of the Creek Indians in Alabama; and should I be correct it need not matter with the Colonel, for you know most people believe a history whether it be correct or not. I have not seen his *History of Alabama*, and all I have seen or heard from him, was his answer to Mr. Hobbs' inquiry; and I have no idea that he has written anything but he felt authorized to do from the sources that he received his information.

But authors sometimes may err, and others willfully misrepresent. When that is the case, we have to judge from circumstances. The Colonel says that Soto (de Soto) passed Alabama before the Muscogees reached that country. The Indians say there were there and fought him: and from the number of copper shields, with a small brass swivel (that an old man by the name of Tooley worked up into bells), would go to show and to prove that the Indians were correct. I have often seen the copper plates or shields, and a piece of the swivel, and from the cuttings or carvings on it, it was evidently of Spanish make. And it was only some twenty years after Cortez conquered Mexico, that Soto (de Soto) commenced his march from Tampa Bay, and had too few men to sacrifice them in storming a strong work, when it could effect nothing, for an Indian Fort in a remote wilderness could have interfered but little with his march westward. And how could the Alabamas have known that he intended passing that way?

It seems to me that a people so illy prepared to build forts; having no axes, spades nor any implement of the sort, would have found it much easier to have concealed themselves, had it been necessary, in some of those large swamps which abound in the Yazoo country; and from what I know of Indians, they would not give one swamp or cane brake for forty forts.

When the Muscogees, Nitches, Choctaws and Chickasaws crossed to the east of the Mississippi river, a town of Indians yet among the Creeks, the Autisees or Itisees, had for ages been called Red Stick. They settled at Baton Rouge, and no doubt it was from that river or town that the early French settlers gave it its present name. Etochatty, signifies red tree or red wood; but ask an Indian that is acquainted with the original names and customs what a Red Stick Warrior, is, and he will tell you it is an Autisee or Otisee. I have taken great pains, in times passed to have these things explained to me by the oldest and most sensible Indians and Indian countrymen. The Muscogees, from their own account, made but a short stay on the Mississippi or its waters. They emigrated to Alabama and Georgia, and settled mostly on the large creeks and rivers and near the falls and shoals, for the purpose of fishing. The Indians who inhabited the Gulf coast, and that of the Atlantic as far east as Beaufort, S.C., and the rivers as far back as latitude 33 north, previous to the settlement of the Muscogees in the country, were known as Paspagolas, Baluxies, Movilas, Apilaches, Hichetas, Uchys, Yemacraws, Wimonsas, Sowanokas or Shawneys. Sowanoka Hatchy is the original name of the Savannah river; that is, the river of the glades.

The Seminoles are a mixed race of almost all the tribes I have mentioned, but mostly Hitchetas and Creeks. The Hitchetas have by the whites been looked upon as being originally Muscogees, but they were not. They had an entirely different language of their own, and were in the country when the Creeks first entered it. Seminole, in the Creek language, signifies wild, or runaway, or outlaw.

You see I write, spell and dictate badly, but have given you what I heard from others who were best calculated to inform me upon such subjects. If there is anything in this that you have not seen or heard before, and you think it worth publishing, do so; if not, let it pass: for I assure you that I am not desirous to become conspicuous as a writer in a newspaper, or anything else— though I doubt much if the man lives that has seen as much of old Indian times, and heard as much of the early history of the Creeks, as I have. I would like to be where I could sit and tell it over to you; I could make you understand it much better.

May you live long and die rich.

T. S. W.

V

WHEELING, WINN PARISH, LA.
MARCH 21, 1858

TO: J. J. HOOPER, Esq.

Dear Sir—Some two weeks back I received the *History of Alabama*, sent to me by my old friend "Horse Shoe Ned." It is a present made me by its Author—whom I have known from his childhood, and of course prize it highly, not only as a present from its author, but for the many new things to me that it contains. I should have commenced this sooner, but my son, who resides near Hot Springs, Arkansas, and the only one of my family that is left me, has been with me for the last three weeks and has just left for his home. That, with my inability to write at best, will make this not very interesting to you or your readers. What I write I dedicate to those that read it. You will see from what I write, and from what I may write hereafter, that I differ from Col. Pickett, and what I write is not intended, nor can it detract in the least from Col. Pickett, as an author, a gentleman, or a scholar. I am not vain enough to think that I could write anything like a history of any country (even if all I write were true) that would be interesting, while Col. Pickett is very capable of doing it; he has not only the advantages of a classical education, but was raised by one of the most intelligent fathers in Alabama; and as to his mother, she has had her equals no doubt, but there is no one living that was her superior. As to my own parents, I can say nothing more than I recollect to have seen them and the only brother I ever had, laid in there last resting place, within six miles of where Savannah river takes its name. My father died in Franklin county, Georgia, near sixty years back; my brother about fifty-six years; my mother about fifty-three years back—leaving an only sister and myself, upon the charity of the best world that I have seen, or any one else, if they will take it right. Now, sir, my whole history through life (thought passing through some pretty rough scenes by-the-by) would not be as interesting as the lives of Washington and Marion, by Old Parson Weems; so I will close my own biography....

You may take almost any other people that we read of and train them to be slaves, or at least make them perform those menial offices that slaves do; but such is never the case with an Indian. It is true, you may, by kind treatment, either in word or action, get them occasionally to perform some little offices; but harsh treatment, either in words or blows, never can control an Indian.

I knew three men in Macon county who could have given Col. Pickett Indian information of modern times (that is, for the last thirty years) which is much more reliable than that he has had. I know something of the settlement of the Tallassee town, opposite Tuckabatchy. I will give you, some time before long, the history of the settlement of Tallassee, and how that error crept into Col. Pickett's *History*.

The three gentlemen alluded to above, in Macon county, are Nat and John Callens and L. B. Strange.

I will here remark, that Col. Pickett's *History* has set me right about the death of Alex. McGillivray. I had thought he died as late as 1796, but I find he died three years before. His daughter and his last wife, who lived by me for many years, could never tell; and if I ever heard from others I forgot it.

I will in my next give you something of the Nitches, Tallassees, and McGillivray's family.

T. S. W.

VI

WHEELING, WINN PARISH, LA.
MARCH 25, 1858

Eds. *Mail*: I see in your paper of March 11th that "J. W. K."
seems desirous to know if I can give the origin of the belief
among the Chippewa Indians—and he presumes among others that there is a deep gulf to be passed after death, before
they can get to their Paradise. I answer him candidly that I
can not and beg to be excused for my profound ignorance on
the subject.

I have never heard of any such belief among those that I
have been acquainted with; and those that I have conversed
with upon religious subjects appeared to have correct notions
of Deity—looked upon Him as an invisible being, who only
made himself known to man through his works. J. W. K.
says in this can be traced a likeness to the Christian belief.
Whence came it? I answer, not from the Jews. Why, not believing the American Indian to be a descendant of the Jew
proves nothing for or against the Christian religion. The
gentleman says there is a marked resemblance in their laws
with regard to marriages that the children of Israel were not

allowed to take wives among other nations, and such was the law among Indians. Such may have been the case—I will not dispute it. But, if such a law ever existed, it was repealed long before my time; and if he will travel among them, and see the number of half-breeds of whites, negroes, and all others that have mixed, and say that the law has not been repealed, I am certain that he will have the candor to admit that it has been grossly violated, at least. There may be something a little alike in the character of the Indian and the Jew, an Indian will sell the shirt off his back for whisky—the Jew will for his money. The Indian, in his wars, often murdered men, women and children, and so did the Jews. By taking the 31st chap. Numbers, and perusing it closely, he will see that I am not mistaken as to the Jews. There was a custom in my time, among Indians, that there were many crimes punishable by their laws—and could the perpetrators of those crimes escape and lay out until their green-corn dance, and then reach the dance-ground undiscovered, they would go unpunished—but in no instance have I ever known murder to go unpunished, if the offender could be caught. The Wind family was allowed—and it was law that they should punish a murder at any and all times—but the other families were not allowed this privilege after a certain time.

T. S. W.

VII

April 2, 1858
F. A. Rutherford, Esq.

Dear Sir;

Your letter of the 8th ultimo, came to hand yesterday. You wish to know something of the early settlement and history of Macon and the adjoining counties.

From what I know of the Indians and their history, I think it as probably as anything that cannot be positively proven, that an occurrence in Macon county caused the Creek Indian war of 1813–14. It was the murder of Arthur Lott, in 1812, by some Chetocchefaula Indians, a branch of the Tallassees. Lott was killed near what is known as the Warrior's Stand. He was moving to the then Mississippi Territory. His family moved on and settled at a bluff on Pearl River, which long went by the name of Lott's Bluff, but is now known as Columbia.

So soon as Col. Hawkins learned that Lott was murdered, he sent Christian Limbo, a German, to Cowetaw, to see Billy McIntosh, a half-breed chief. (For the following, see *Servants on Horses*.) From Cowetaw, Limbo and McIntosh went to Thleacatska or Broken Arrow, to see Little Prince. The Prince was too old for active service, and sent a well-known half-breed, George Lovet, who was also a chief. Lovet took with him some Cussetas and McIntosh some Cowetas, and accompanied Limbo to Tuckabatchy to see the Big Warrior. He placed some Tuckabatchy under a chief called Emutta and the celebrated John McQueen, a negro, and all under the control of McIntosh, went in pursuit of the murderers. They found them on the Notasulga creek, at a place known since as Williamson Ferrell's settlement: where they shot the leaders and returned to their respective towns. This act aroused the Tallassees, and James McQueen, who had controlled them for 95 years having died the year before, his influence was lost, and from talks made sometime before by Tucumseh the Sowanaka or Shawanee, and Seekaboo, a Warpicanata chief and prophet, (who was afterwards at the destruction of Ft. Mims,) a number of the young warriors and a few of the old ones had become restless. Not long after Lott was killed, an old gentleman named Merideth was killed at the crossing on Catoma creek, in what is now Montgomery county. This was done by the Otisees in a drunken spree. The Big Warrior undertook to have them punished, but failed to do so, and in attempting to arrest them an Otisse was killed. A few days after this, the Otisees attacked a party of Tuckabachys, under the chief Emutta, at the Old Agency or Polecat Springs, which was then occupied by Nimrod Doyle. Doyle had been a soldier under Gen. St. Clair, was at his defeat and afterwards with Gen. Wayne.

About this time, or a little after, a chief, Tustanuggachee or Little Warrior, and a Coowersortda Indian, known as Capt. Isaacs, who had gone north-west with Tucumseh, were returning to the Creek nation, and learned from some Chickasaws that the Creeks had gone to war. Relying on this information, the Little Warrior's party did some mischief on the frontier of Tennessee as well as killed a few persons. On their return to the nation they found that war had not actually broken out, but only the few little depredations that I have mentioned, had been committed. The Coowersortda Indians, Capt. Sam. Isaacs (a name he borrowed from an old trader who died some years back in Lincoln county, Tenn., and who was one of the most cunning, artful scamps I ever saw among the Indians), gave the Big Warrior information about the murders in Tennessee. Isaacs from his tricks and management and having Alexander McGillivray's[1] daughter for a wife, was let out of the scrape; but the Little Warrior being a Hickory-Ground Indian, set the Coosa Indians at variance with big Warrior. After this the Tuckabatchys, Ninny-pask-ulgees, or Road Indians, the Chunnanuggees and Conaligas all forted in, at Tuckabatchy, to defend themselves from those that had turned hostile.

I have often heard Sam Moniac say, that if Lott had not been killed at the time he was, it was his belief that war could have been prevented. He and Billy Weatherford (See *Servants on Horses*) have often said to me as well as others, that the Big Warrior at the time Tucumseh made his talk at Tuckabatchy, was inclined to take the talk, and at heart, was as hostile as any, if he had not been a coward. I have no doubt, from what I have heard Weatherford say, he (W) was as much opposed to that war as any one living: but when it was necessary to take sides, he went with his countrymen, and gave me his reasons for so doing. He said, to join the whites was a thing he did not think right, and had it been so they would not have thanked him, and would have attributed it to cowardice. Besides, he said to remain with his people, he could prevent his misguided countrymen from committing many depredations that they might otherwise do. Weatherford was never a chief, though

---

1 There are two Alexander McGillivrays. The first (1759–1793), son of a Scottish trader and a Creek woman, educated in Charleston, fought for Indian unity, maintained Creeks were a separate nation, denied validity of treaties with Georgia, joined Spanish in Florida after claims were denied, later negotiated treaty with George Washington for better terms.

exercising as much or more influence over a part of the nation than many that were chiefs. He did not act the part which some writers say he did in the war, thought I think he was fully as great a man as any have made him out to be. He was of a different order of man to what has generally been believed. As I knew him well and have had as good opportunities to become acquainted with his history and character, as most men that now live, I will, when I have leisure, give you Gen. Jackson and Col. Hawkins' opinion of the man, and what I think to be a more correct history than anything I have seen written about him: and should any one doubt my judgment about him, none that knew these men will doubt theirs.

VIII

WHEELING, WINN PARISH
APRIL 25, 1858

COL. ALBERT PICKETT,

Dear Sir:

Your letter of the 23rd February last, addressed to me through *The Montgomery Mail*, reached me some weeks since, and I have been too much engaged to write, had I been able to write anything worth reading, or to answer your inquiry about the Uchees and their language. All I can say about them is, that they occupied portions of Alabama, Georgia, and perhaps South Carolina.

As I have before stated, a number of the Uchees went North-West with the Shawnees, many years ago. And not long after they reached their new homes on the waters of the Ohio, they commenced their depredations on the frontier settlers of Virginia and Pennsylvania. In one of their scouts they captured a white boy on the frontier of Pennsylvania, by the name of John Hague. This boy Hague was raised to manhood among them, and proved to be as great a savage as any of them. He took an Uchee woman for a wife and raised a number of children: it was also said that Hague raised an illegitimate son by a white woman named Girthy or Girty, and called his name Simon Girty, after his mother.

I do not know that it would be slandering the illustrious dead to say that Jack was the Marchal Ney of the old hostile Indians: Jack fought through the war, and after their defeat at Horse Shoe, and Gen. Jackson moved his troops to the place where he built Fort Jackson, the Indians then became very much discouraged and commenced coming in. The chiefs who had controlled these towns during the War could get in striking distance, to hear what was to be done. Jack sent his women and children out of the head waters of Catoma, and secreted his warriors between a cane brake and the river, not far above the present city of Montgomery. Weatherford, who was not a chief (but had more influence than many who were), placed his people on a little island in the Alabama river, near the mouth of Noland creek, that makes into the river on the North or Autauga side, known as Moniac's Island. Weatherford's people were Tuskegees. Peter McQueen and his Talassees quartered themselves upon the head waters of Line creek. John and Sandy Durant, the brothers of McQueen's wife, and also the brothers of Lochlin Durant, that you know, remained with McQueen. Josiah Francis, the Prophet, Nehe Marthla Micco, the Otisee chief (both of them hanged, 1818, by Gen. Jackson), placed their people not far above the Federal crossing on the Catoma. Hossa Yoholo, a very white half-breed chief, and a son by a man named of Powell, I think, took shelter in a dense cane forest in the bend opposite Montgomery. This man, from what I have learned, was one of the most reckless fighters in the nation. Ogillis Ineha, or Menauway, who was the principal leader at Horse Shoe, and at the time was supposed to be killed, carried his people near the falls of Cahawba, where he remained for more than a year after peace was made.

This was the situation of those chiefs and their people about the time and shortly after General Jackson reached Franca Choka Chula, or the old French trading-house, as it was called by the Indians. Weatherford sent up old Tom Carr, or Tuskegee Emarthla, and he soon learned through Sam Moniac, his brother-in-law (who was always friendly), that he was in no danger, and so he came to camp (but not in the way it has been represented). General Jackson, as if by intuition, seemed to know that Weatherford was no savage and much more than an ordinary man by nature, and treated him very kindly indeed.

Savannah Jack, or, as he has been called by some, Sowanoka Jack, was not then as well known to the whites as many others. He frequented the camp pretty much unnoticed (no doubt as he wished to be). It was not long before it was understood that Jacksa Chula Harjo (as the Indians used to call Gen. Jackson) wanted land to pay for the trouble he had been at, and the Big Warrior and others were in favor of giving Old Mad Jackson, as they called him, as much land as he wanted. Jack poor fellow—his little field happened to be on the Montgomery side of Line creek, and of course would have to go with the ceded territory. This Jack could not stand; he threatened to kill the Big Warrior and go to fighting the whites again. It was soon understood that a hostile chief was in camp, making threats, and the General wished to see him; but Jack disappeared. He took his warriors from the cypress brake near Montgomery, went out to Catoma, where his women and children were, and there joined Francis and the Otisee chief.

Hoosa Yoholo left the bend of the river at Montgomery and joined Jack and his crowd, as also did McQueen and the Durants. The boy, Billy Powell, who was the grandson of one of Peter McQueen's sisters, was then but a little boy, and was with this party. They all put out for Florida, and on their route they split among themselves. Jack and his people being Uchees and Sowanokas, called a halt on the Sepulga, about there and on the line of West Florida, where he remained until he went West.

McQueen and the others went to East Florida. Sandy Durant died at Tampa Bay, not long after they reached that country. John Durant went to Nassau, on the Island of New Providence. Peter McQueen remained in Florida until after Gen. Jackson's campaign of 1818, shortly after which he died on a little barren island on the Atlantic side of Cape Florida. Hossa Yoholo, the white half-breed chief, died on Indian river in East Florida, with a disease in his feet caused from an insect there known as the jigger. This I learned from a hostile negro who was raised with a family by the name of Powell, but in after times was known as Holmes' Ned. He accompanied Hossa Yoholo or the Singling Sun to Florida. I knew Ned many years: I purchased him from our friend, Horse Shoe Ned, and he died mine.

I will try and account to you for an error that many have fallen into, about Billy Powell, or Oceola. As I remarked before, this boy went with his uncle, McQueen, to Florida. I knew him well after that, and have seen him frequently. Capt. Isaac Brown and myself, with a party of friendly Creeks and Uchees, made him a prisoner in 1818, and he was then but a lad.

T. S. W

IX

WHEELING, WINN PARISH, LA.
JUNE 13, 1858

J. J. HOOPER, Esq:

Dear Sir,

Some years before the Creek war, and when I was quite a youngster, I made occasional visits to the Ocmulgee river, which was then the line between the whites and the Indians. The Indians claimed half the river, and spring or shad-catching time the Indians would flock from all parts of the nation in great numbers to the Ocmulgee. They could be seen at every shoal as high up the river as shad could run, down to the Altamaha, for the purpose of fishing. On one of my trips to Old Fort Hawkins, I became acquainted with an Indian countryman by the name of John Ward; and for the first time I ever visited the Creek agency, which was then on Flint River was in company with Ward, an old uncle of mine, and one Andrew McDougald. Col. Hawkins was then holding a council with some chiefs from various parts of the nation. I met with Ward occasionally from that time until the war commenced. When Gen. Floyd moved his troops to Flint River, Ward was the interpreter for the officer in command at Fort Manning. He then came into Gen. Floyd's camp, and remained with the army until it reached the Chattahoochee, and commenced building Fort Mitchell. He was often sent out with Nimrod Doyle as a spy. There was also an Indian countryman along by the name of Bob Mosely. Moseley's wife was the niece of Peter McQueen. Ward's wife was a relation of Daniel McDonald, more generally known to the whites as Daniel McGillivray, and both of their wives were then with the hostile Indians. Ward and Moseley seemed willing to risk any and everything to forward the movements of the army, in order to reach the neighborhood of their families.

There was a detachment of soldiers sent out to Uchee creek, to throw up a breastwork. I was one of the party. Among the rest was a Baptist preacher by the name of Elisha Moseley, a very sensible and most excellent man at that, and as grave as men ever get to be; for he could pray all night and fight all day, or pray all day and fight all night, just as it came his turn to do either; and this preacher was a brother to Bob Moseley, the Indian countryman.

While at this breastwork, one night, by a campfire, I listened to Elijah Moseley inquiring into his brother's motives for leaving a white family and making his home among a tribe of savages. Bob's reply was, as well as I now recollect, that there was no false swearing among Indian. The preacher then commenced making some enquiry into Ward's history. Ward informed him that his father had taken him into the Creek nation…when he (Ward) was a child, and shortly after died, and that he recollected very little of his father; that he had been raised by Daniel McDonald, or McGillivray, as he was commonly called, that he heard McDonald say that his father was a Georgian, and had left a wife and children in that State. ….Some one in the camp, that had heard of Ward's father quitting his family and disappearing with one of his children, and knowing something of the Wards in Georgia, looked at John Ward and said, from the near resemblance of him and a Georgia Word, they must be brothers.

The Georgia brother was written to, and in a few weeks, made his appearance in camp. In this time, the Indian Ward, from exposure, had fallen sick, and was very low. The Georgia brother came into camp one night, and the next morning John Ward was a corpse—though John was perfectly rational on the arrival of his brother and, before he died knew who he was. They proved to be twin brothers. Ward died in one of the tents of Adams' riflemen, and Elijah Moseley was his nurse. The most feeling pulpit talk I ever heard dropped from the lips of Elijah Moseley, in a soldier's tent, on the death of John Ward.

I will close this by saying to you, that I wrote another letter to Col. Pickett, trying to prove to him that I was better acquainted with Indian history than himself; but not knowing whether the first was published, I decline sending it, thinking it probable that they were getting too long and uninteresting for publication; and, from my manner of writing, I could give no satisfaction—if satisfaction I could give at all—and have them much shorter.

Yours,

T. S. W.

X

(Editor's note: The letter below was inserted into General Woodward's Reminiscenses and his reply to the writer, Colonel John Banks, follows.)

From the *Columbus (Ga.) Sun.*

Eds. *Sun*: In the spring of 1818, the writer was in Gen. Jackson's army, in Florida, consisting of near 4,000 men, including regulars commanded by Gen. Gaines; Georgia militia commanded by Gen. Glascock; the Tennessee horsemen and friendly Indians under Gen. McIntosh. Major Thomas Woodward and Captain Isaac Brown had a kind of joint command with McIntosh over the Indians.

While marching between St. Marks, and Sewannee Town, distance about one hundred miles, on Sunday, the 12th day of April, we discovered fresh signs of Indians.

Gen. McIntosh, with his command of Creek Indians, pursued them The main army, as was our habit, lay down in the grass to rest and await McIntosh return. Very soon McIntosh over took them and the battle commenced in hearing of us, probably a mile off. We could hear the firing of guns, which continued for some time.

Well, I remember an express borne from McIntosh. An Indian, on foot, running, crying out at the top of his voice, "Captain Jackson, Captain Jackson." As he passed us, we pointed to Old Hickory, who soon dispatched a company of Tennessee mounted men to aid McIntosh. The battle was finished ere they reached him. McIntosh and Woodward soon returned to our camp with their prisoners, consisting of women and children, and a white woman to our surprise. This woman is still living in or about Fort Gaines. She was then Mrs. Stuart, and afterwards married John Dill, of Fort Gaines, who died a few years since.

For the particulars of her capture by the Indians and recapture by McIntosh and Woodward, I refer to the enclosed letter, which I have just received from Gen. Woodward, which, if you think of sufficient interest, please copy in full, or make such extracts as you choose. Since receiving this letter from Gen. Woodward, I have hunted up my diary, kept during that campaign, and have made the above extract.

XI

WHEELING, WINN PARISH, LA.
June 16th, 1858

COL. JOHN BANKS:

Dear Sir:

Your letter of the 27th ult. is as welcome as it was unexpected. Anything from those I knew in early life is consoling to my feelings in my present lonely situation, particularly when it contains such kindly expressed feelings for my welfare here and my happiness hereafter. In your P. S. you say I may have forgotten you. Your name is a familiar one to me, and it is possible I may not know which one of that name I am writing to, but it would be treating unkindly one of the best memories that man ever had to doubt it. If you are the John Banks I think I am writing to, you were born in Georgia, and the same county I was, Elbert.

In 1818 there were two companies of soldiers from Elbert county, Ga., one commanded by Capt. Mann; the other by Capt. Ashley. You were a Lieutenant in one of them. I remember the trip to Fort Early that you speak of, as I do most of what occurred in that Florida expedition. That was a little over forty years ago. The names you mention in your letter are as familiar to me as my own. The two women whose names you mention, if the incidents connected with their lives were as well-known to some as they are to myself, would afford material for a very interesting book. Mrs. Stuart (now Mrs. Dill) you saw when Capt. Brown and myself carried her to your camp; you know something of her history—at least you know something of her being a captive among the hostile Indians. And as I have nothing to do today, and you live in Columbus among many of my old acquaintances as well as relatives, and perhaps some of them would be willing to hear that I am living at least, I will give you a little of their (Mrs. Dill's and Mrs. Brown's) history.

In 1816 and 1817, the Florida Indians were doing mischief, and the Government found it necessary to keep troops quartered on the borders of Florida. Fort Scott and Fort Huse were erected to protect the settlers in Early county, Georgia. That was then a new and thinly settled country. The command of the troops was given to Colonel Arbuckle. He had frequent skirmishes with the Indians, under the control of Chitto-Fanna-Chula, or old Snake Bone, but known to you and the whites generally as old Ne-he-mathla. Supplies for the troops had to be carried from New Orleans and Mobile by water. A very large boat with army stores was started from Mobile Point. Mrs. Stuart was among those on board; her husband, a Sergeant, and a fine looking man at that, had gone with the troops by land. The boat, having to be propelled by oars and poles was long on the trip, and by this time, the war had completely opened. The old hostile Creeks, from various parts of Florida, were engaged in it; among others the two Chiefs you saw hanged at St. Mark's—Josiah Francis and Ne-he-mathla Micco. They headed a party and watched the boats. As those on board were hooking and jamming (as the boatmen called it) near the bank and opposite a thick canebrake, the Indians fired on them, killing and wounding most of those on board at the first fire. Those not disabled from the first fire of the Indians made the best fight they could, but all on board were killed except Mrs. Stuart and two soldiers Gray, and another man whose name I have forgot, if I ever knew it; they were both shot, but they made their escape by swimming to the opposite shore.

Mrs. Stuart was taken almost lifeless as well as senseless, and was a captive until the day I carried her to your camp. After taking her from the boat, they (the Indians) differed among themselves as to whose slave or servant she should be. An Indian by the name of Yellow Hair said he had many years before been sick at or near St. Mary's, and that he felt it was a duty to take the woman and treat her kindly, as he was treated so by a white woman when he was among the whites. The matter was left to an old Indian by the name of Bear Head, who decided in favor of Yellow Hair. I was told by the Indians that Yellow Hair treated her with great kindness and respect. I never asked her any questions as to her treatment, and presume she never knew me from any other Indian, as Brown and myself were both dressed like Indians. We knew long before we recaptured her band she was with, and had tried to come up with them before.

The most tiresome march I ever made was one night in company with the present Gen. Twiggs. He with some soldiers and I with a party of Indians, trying to rescue her at old Tallahassee, but the Indians had left before we reached the place. I shall never, while I live, forget the day we took her from the Indians. Billy Mitchell, a son of the then Indian agent, Brown, Kendall Lewis, John Winslett, Sam. Hail and myself were the only white men that were with the Indians, except old Jack Carter, my pack-horseman. The white men I have named and the Hitchetas trader Noble Kenard, and the

Uchees under Timpoochy Bernard, commenced the fight.

Shortly after the firing commenced, we could hear a female voice in the English language calling for help, but she was concealed from our view. The hostile Indians, though greatly inferior in number to our whole force, had the advantage of the ground, it being a dense thicket, and kept the party that first attacked at bay until Gen. McIntosh arrived with the main force. McIntosh, though raised among savages, was a General; yes, he was one of God's make of Generals. I could hear his voice above the din of firearms "Save the white woman! Save the Indian women and children!" All this time Mrs. Stuart was between the fires of the combatants. McIntosh said to me: "Chulatarla Emathla, you, Brown and Mitchell, go that woman." (Chulatarla Emathla was the name I was known by among the Indians.)

Mitchell was a good soldier and a bad cripple from rheumatism. He dismounted from his horse and said: "Boys, let me lead the way." We made the charge with some Uchees and Creeks, but Mitchell, poor fellow, was soon left behind, in consequence of his inability to travel on foot. I can see her now, squatted in the saw palmetto, among a few dwarf cabbage trees, surrounded by a group of Indian women. There I saw Brown kill an Indian, and I got my rifle stock shot off just back of the lock. Old Jack Carter came up with my horse shortly after we cut off the woman from the warriors. I got his musket and used it until the fight ended. You saw her (Mrs. Stuart) when she reached the camp, and recollect her appearance better than I can describe it.

By the time you get through what I have scribbled, I reckon you will be a little cautious how you write to your old Indian acquaintances who have little else to do than sit and think over old times. You say you reckon I am not an old man; you are right. Time, the common leveler of our race, has not passed me unnoticed, and according to the course of things it will not

70

be a great while before I am turned over to the terror of kings. If you see Jack or Thacker Howard, tell them I am living. May you live as long as suits your convenience.

Respectfully,

T. S. W.

XII

WHEELING, WINN PARISH, LA.
JUNE 21, 1858

COL. A. J. PICKETT:

Dear Sir:
In your letter to me of February last, you mentioned something of the inquiry I made in a private letter to my friend Hartrick, about a manuscript. Why that inquiry was made, I had learned that you had had, at one time, the manuscripts of George Stiggins, and possibly I might learn something of the manuscript I loaned him. I had no idea that anything I had written would be used by you, or anyone else, in the history of a country; but the manuscript of Christian Limbo, taken from Col. Hawkins writings, I would have been glad to have gotten hold of, as it contained much I think (if now published) that would be new to you and others, and entertaining to all who take an interest in Indian history.

Besides, it contained the copies of two letters written as far back as 1735, by Sir James or Gen. Oglethorpe. They were written at different times, but both written at Frederica, on St. Simond's Island. The letters were directed to James McQueen,

72

requesting him to use his influence with the Indians and prevent them, if possible, from taking sides with the Spaniards who were then threatening to attack the infant colony of Georgia. The letters were written in a style very different from letters written at the present day; and the bearer of those letters was a Scotchman named Malcolm McPherson. He was the natural father of Sehoya, or Schoy McPherson, and she was the mother of Davy Tate and Billy Weatherford, and was not the daughter of Lauchlan McGillivray, as has been represented.

McPherson was the man that gave Lauchlan McGillivray his first start as a trader.[1] McGillivray came into the Creek nation in company with John Tate and Daniel McDonald. John Tate was the father of Davy Tate and was the last agent the English Government ever had among the Creeks. During the American Revolution, Tate raised a large number of Indians on the waters of the Alabama, and from almost every town (except the Tallassees and Netchez, who, through the influence of McQueen, never did take up arms against the colonies during the revolution).

Tate carried his warriors to Chattahoochee, and there joined Tusta Nuggy Hopoy, or Little Prince, with the Chattahoochee Indians, and started to Augusta, Ga., to aid a Col. Griefson, better known as Grayson, a Tory Colonel. Near the head springs of the Upatoy creek, and near Fort Perry, Tate became deranged; the cause I never learned. He was brought back to old Cusscrawa and died; he was buried on a high hill east of the old town, and near what was the residence of Gen. Woolfolk when I left the country. I have been shown his grave often, and have heard what I have stated from Little Prince, and a hundred others that were along at the time. When Tate died, the Alabama Indians mostly returned, except the Tuckabatchys under Efau

---

1 The persons General Woodward is speaking of here were early settlers of Alabama/Georgia and were involved with the indigenous Creeks during the American Revolution.

Tustanuggy, or Dog Warrior. (He was known to the whites as Davy Cornels; he was the father of the present speaker of the Creeks, Hopoithleyohola, and a brother of Alexander McGillivray's last wife.) This man with his warriors accompanied the Little Prince and his party to Augusta, and did some fighting and much other mischief.

This man Davy Cornels did more mischief to the whites than any man that has lived among the Creeks, and was the most hostile and better enemy the whites ever had among the Creeks, Savannah Jack excepted. While Seagrove was agent, Cornels sent him word he wished to be at peace and would visit him at Colerain, near St. Mary's. It was known to some that Seagrove was expecting a visit from Davy Cornels—a James Harrison that had suffered much by the Indians, waylaid Cornels' path and killed him, bearing a white flag.

We might go back to Laughlan McGillivray; he was a Scotchman, as was Tate. And not long before or after Tate had left the nation for Augusta, McGillivray took his two children, Sophy and Alexander, and started for Savannah; the Americans lay about Col. Campbell's camp or fort in such numbers that he was forced to send his children back to the nation by his negro man Charles. Charles lived with and about me for years, and I have heard him and others who corroborated his statement, tell it often. Sophy was the oldest of the two. So, you see, you and I differ widely as to the time Alexander McGillivray came into existence, because Alex. McGillivray's mother was not the daughter of a Frenchman or French soldier. She was a full blooded Tuskegee Indian. Your history says Alexander was the first born of Lauchlan MccGillivray and Sehoy Marchand. I speak nothing but the truth when I tell you that I know my opportunities for information on this subject have been much better than yours, and that Sophy was the oldest child and an own sister to Alexander, and that will do away with the dream of so much books and papers.

Your history says that the mother of Tate and Weatherford was a sister to Alexander McGillivray. I will now tell you how you have been led into that error; I see you speak of the Wind tribe of Indians, and I also see that you give Barrent Deboys' versions of it; he never could tell the difference between clan as family and a tribe. I have before this, in one of my letters to Mr. Hooper tried to explain this family arrangement. The Creek Indians were laid off in families or clans, as were the Scots with their Campbells, McPhersons, McGregers, and so on, with this difference; The Scotch clans had just as many privileges as their numbers and the strength of their arms would allow them. The privileges of the Indian clans were prescribed by their laws, but the Wind family or clan were always allowed more than the Bears, Panthers, Foxes and others; and any of these families in speaking of the family to which he or she belonged, claimed kin with the whole family as brother, sister, uncle, aunt, and at the same time be no ways related by blood.

And as to what family Tate and McGillivray's wives belonged, I do not pretend to say, thought I am certain that's the way the relationship has come about. For I never heard of the mother of McGillivray being crossed upon the French until I saw it in your history. But always understood her to be a full Indian, and the mother of Tate and Weatherford to be a half-breed, and the most interesting woman in the nation of her time.

I see in your history, for the first time I ever heard of such a thing, that Alexander McGillivray was an educated man. (Editor's note: At the time, to be educated meant to be conversant with the Latin and Greek languages and literature.) That's new to me as it would have been to himself, could he have been shown it in his day. The letters purporting to have been written by him which appear in the *History of Alabama*, are well written, and show conclusively that they emanated

75

from no ordinary man. But could the author of those letters and McGillivray to whom they are ascribed, look back, they could say that the world is yet as credulous as in their time. If there is any one living that can or could identify the hand writing of a Scotchman by the name of Alex F. Leslie, he could easily tell who wrote those letters. This man Leslie did McGillivray's writing and was worthy of (so far as intellect is concerned) the notice of his distinguished relative of our own country, General Alexander Hamilton.

I never knew McGillivray, but I think I know his true character as well as any now living, as I have mingled much with both whites and Indians that knew him well. As I once wrote to a gentleman before I ever saw your history, had Alexander McGillivray been living in the war of 1813 and '14, and could have united his people the history of that war would have been a very different one to what it is. I know it was the opinion of Gen. Washington that McGillivray acted with duplicity towards our government, and you in your history give the reader to think that he was a treacherous man. But I differ with your history as I do with the best man that left his name on record, as to McGillivray's true character. I know that McGillivray never liked our people or our government, but that he carried out every promise that he ever made, in good faith too, I have no doubt. I have learned this from those that knew him—knew his feelings, and the awkward situation he was placed in, and what he had contended with. He had to deal more or less with the United States, England, and Spain, all three jealous of McGillivray, and all jealous of each other; it would have taken a man North of Mason and Dixon's line to wear a face to have suited all those that McGillivray had to deal with and make any thing of a fair show.

I knew Davy Tate well and spent near seven weeks with him at one time, many years ago; he was decidedly the most sensible and well informed man I have ever seen of the Indian blood (that is the Creek) he was not educated; a man of much truth, and like his half-brother, a man of great firmness. He has talked to me much; I never heard him say the McGillivray was a man of letters. But he has often said to me that McGillivray lived pretty much upon the property of his (Tate's) father, and that the man Daniel McDonald, that I have before spoken of who came to the country with Lauchlan McGillivray and John Tate, that after the disappearance of Lauchlan McGillivray from the country, he (Daniel McDonald) assumed the name of Daniel McGillivray, and fell heir to most of McGillivray's property that he left in the nation. This I have heard from others, as well as from Davy Tate. This man Daniel McDonald, or Daniel McGillivray, was the father of the chief known as Bit Nose Billy McGillivray.

I knew Alexander McGillivray's children well; his daughter Peggy was the wife of Charles Cornels, and died before Cornels hung himself. His daughter Lizzy lived by me for years; I purchased hers and her son's land. They were located on section 16, in township 16 and range 24; it lies in Macon county, near Tuskegee. I sold it to James Dent. I lived many years by Mrs. McGirth; who was McGillivray's last wife; spoke good English,—from none of these did I hear he was a scholar.

I could say much more upon this subject, but this is already too long. I will close this by saying to you, that as you and I both have had to rely upon the statements of others for what we write, and you much more than myself, we will remain as we always have been, friends, and let those that read what we write judge which is most likely to be right. When I have time I will write and point out many errors that you have been led into that I know of my own knowledge, and come within the knowledge of others that still live. It is our nature when we say or write a thing, to wish the world to believe us right (and many wish it if they know they are wrong). But there is nothing more noble and generous in a man, than when he finds he is in error to own and abandon it. And as there has been some little interest taken or felt in what I have written, if I can I will spend a month or two in Montgomery next winter. I could tell you many things that have been forgotten, and could point out many places that would interest you and others that are living there.

Yours, &c.

T. S. W.

XIII

WHEELING, WINN PARISH, LA.
JULY 8, 1858

J. J. HOOPER. Esq.

Dear Sir:

The entry of Gen. LaFayette into Alabama, was the most imposing show I witnessed while I lived in the State. In 1824, I think it was, LaFayette was looked for in Alabama. I was the first and oldest Brigadier General in Alabama, (after it became a State). Gen. Wm. Taylor, I think, was the oldest Major General; and Israel Pickens was Governor. There may have been his superior in that office since Alabama became a State. At the time LaFayette was expected, Gen. Taylor was absent, I think, in Mobile. The Indians were a little soured, from a treaty that had been made with the Georgians. Gov. Pickens requested me to take an escort and conduct LaFayette through the nation. The Hon. James Abercrombie then commanded the Montgomery Troop, and Gen. Moore of Claiborne, commanded the Monroe Troop, both of whom volunteered their services. Before the escort left Alabama (which then extended only to Line Creek), Gen. Taylor arrived and took the command.

That was before the day of platforms and conventions—men lived on their own money. You must guess then there was some patriotic feelings along, for there were between two and three hundred persons, all bearing their own expenses. Some in going and coming had to travel four hundred miles, and none less than two hundred miles. Besides the military, there were a number of most respectable citizens of Alabama—among whom were Boling Hall, ex-member of Congress, ex-Governor Murphy, John D. Bibb, John W. Freeman and Col. James Johnson, one of the best men that ever lived or died. If there are any such men these days, I have not had the pleasure of their acquaintance. Our trip to the Cattahoochee was pleasant indeed.

We made our headquarters three miles from Fort Mitchell, on big Uchee Creek, at Haynes Crabtree's. Had that been a war, and if it had continued till the present day, all of that crowd that's now living would be soldiers. After some three or four day's stay at Crabtree's, we learned that Gen. LaFayette had passed White Water, and we knew at what time he would reach the river. The Indians seemed to take as much interest in the matter as the whites. All hands mustered on the west of Alabama side, where we could see the Georgia escort approach the east bank of the Chattahooche, with their charge. On the east bank, Gen. Lafayette was met by Chilly McIntosh, son of the Indian Gen. McIntosh, with fifty Indian warriors, who were stripped naked and finely painted. They had a sulky prepared with drag-ropes, such as are commonly used in drawing cannon. The General was turned over by the Georgians to the Indians. That was the greatest show I ever saw at the crossing of any river. It beat all of Gen. Jessup's wind bridges across the Tallapoosa, and other places where there was never much more water than would swim a dog, only at high rise. As the ferry-boat reached the Alabama side, the Indians, in two lines, seized the ropes, and the General seated in the sulky, was drawn to the top of the bank, some eighty yards, where stood the Alabama Delegation. At a proper distance from the Alabama delegation, the Indians opened their lines and the sulky halted.

Everything, from the time the General entered the ferry, till this time, had been conducted in the most profound silence. As the sulky halted, the Indians gave three loud whoops. The General then alighted, took off his hat, and was conducted by Chilly McIntosh, a few steps, to where stood Mr. Hall, with head uncovered, white with the frost of age. I knew Mr. Hall from my boyhood. He always showed well in company; but never did I see him look so finely, as on that occasion—he looked like himself—what he really was—an American gentleman. As McIntosh approached Mr. Hall, he said, "Gen. Lafayette, the American friend"—"Mr. Hall, of Alabama," pointing to each as he called his name. Mr. Hall, in a very impressive manner, welcomed LaFayette to the shores of Alabama, and introduced him to the other gentlemen. Dandridge Bibb then addressed the General at some length. I heard a number of persons address LaFayette on his route through Alabama—none surpassed Dandridge Bibb, and none equaled him, unless it was Hitchcock and Dr. Hustis at Cahaba. I have always been looked on as rather dry-faced; but gazing on the face of the most distinguished patriot that it had ever fallen to my lot to look upon, and feeling remarks of Mr. Bibb on that occasion, caused me, as it did most others that were present, to shed tears like so many children.

After the address at the river, all marched to Fort Mitchell hill, where there was an immense crowd of Indians, the Little Prince at their head. He addressed the "French Captain," through Hamley, in true Indian style. I could understand much of his speech, but cannot begin to give it as Mamley could. The Prince said that he had often heard of the "French Captain," but now I see him, I take him by the hand, I know from what I see, he is the true one I have heard spoken of; I am not deceived—too many men have come a long way to meet him. He is bound to be the very man the Americans were looking for. The Prince, after satisfying the General that he (the Prince) was satisfied that the General was the true man spoken of and looked for, then went on to say, that he had once warred against the Americans, and the French Captain had warred for them, and of course they had once been enemies, but were now friends; that he (the Prince) was getting old, which his withered limbs would show—making bare his arms at the same time—that he could not live long; but he was glad to say, that his people and the whites were at peace and he hoped they would continue so.

But he had raised a set of young warriors, that he thought would prove worthy of their sires, if there should ever be a call to show themselves men; and as a ball play was, outside of war, the most manly exercise that the Red Man could perform, he would, for the gratification of the General and his friends, make his young men play a game. The old man then turned to his people, and said to them—they were in presence of a great man and warrior; he had commanded armies on both sides of the Big Water; that he had seen many nations of people; that he had visited Six Nations, in Red Jacket's time (the General told the Indians that he had visited the Six Nations) that every man must do his best—show himself a man, and should one get hurt he must retire without complaining, and by no means show anything like ill humor. The speech ended, about two hundred stripped to the buff, paired themselves off and went at it. It was a ball play sure enough, and I would travel farther to see such a show than I would to see any other performed by man, and willingly pay high for it, at that. The play ended, and all hands went out to head quarters at Big Uchee, where we were kindly treated by our old friend Haynes Crabtree.

There was a man then living among the Indians, Capt. Tom Anthony, who long since found a last resting place in the wilds of Arkansas. He was a man of fine sense and great humor. There was also an Indian known as Whiskey John. John was the greatest drunkard I ever saw; he would drink a quart of strong whiskey without taking the vessel that contained it from his lips, (this is Alabama history, and there are plenty now living that have seen him do it). To see John drink was enough to have made the fabled Bacchus look out for a vacancy that frequently occurs among the Sons of Temperance. Capt. Anthony told John that all hands had addressed the French Chief, and that it was his duty to say something to him on behalf of those that loved whiskey. John could speak considerable English in a broken manner. It so happened that the General and others were walking across the Uchee Bridge when John met them. John made a low bow, as he had seen others do. The General immediately pulled off his hat, thinking he had met with another chief. John, straightening himself up to his full height (and he was not very low), commenced his speech in the manner that I will try to give it to you. "My friend, you French Chief? me Whiskey John," (calling over the names of several persons and Indians) "Col. Hawkins, Col Crowell, Tom Crowell, Henry Crowell, Billy McIntosh, Big Warrior Indian, heap my friends, give me whiskey, drink, am good. White man my very good friend me, white man make whiskey, drink him heap, very good, I drink whiskey. You French Chief. Tom Anthony say me big Whiskey Chief. You me give one bottle full. I drink him good." The General informed John that he did not drink whiskey, but would have his bottle filled. John remarked, "Tom Anthony you very good man, me you give bottle full. You no drink, me drink him all, chaw tobacco little bit, give me some you."

Now the above is an Indian Speech, and no doubt will appear silly to some who have not been accustomed to those people. Should it, however fall under the eye of those who were along at the time, they will recognize John's speech, and call to mind our old friends, Capt. Anthony and Col James Johnson, who was the life of our crowd.

We remained that night at Crabtree's and the next day reached Fort Bainbridge, where an Indian countryman lived, by the name of Kendall Lewis, as perfect a gentleman, in principle, as ever lived in or out of the nation, and had plenty, and in fine style. The next day we started for Line Creek.

It fell my lot to point out many Indians, as well as places, for we were stopped at almost every settlement to shake hands, and hear Indian speeches. Every thing was "done up" better than it will ever be again; one thing only was lacking—time—we could not stay long enough. The next morning we started for Montgomery. Such a cavalcade never traveled that road before or since.

On Goat Hill, and near where Capt. John Carr fell in the well, stood Gov. Pickens, and the largest crowd I ever saw in Montgomery. Some hundred yards east of the Hill, was sand flat, where Gen. LaFayette and his attendants quit carriages and horses, formed a line and marched to the top of the hill. As we started, the band struck up the old Scottish air, "Hail to the Chief." As we approached the Governor, Mr. Hill introduced the General to him. The Governor tried to welcome him, but like the best man the books give account of, when it was announced that he was commander of the whole American forces, he was scarcely able to utter a word. So it was with Gov. Pickens. As I remarked before, Gov. P. had no superior in the State, but on that occasion he could not even make a speech. But that did not prevent Gen. LaFayette from discovering that he was a great man; it only goes to prove what is often said, that many who feel the most can say least, and many who have no feeling say too much.

The people of Montgomery did their duty. Col. Arthur Hayne, who was a distinguished officer in the army the war of 1813, and who was the politest gentleman I ever saw, was the principal manager. If the Earl of Chesterfield had happened there he would have felt as I did the first time I saw a fine carpet on a floor and was asked to walk in; I declined, saying, "I reckon I got in the wrong place." Several steamboats were in waiting at the wharf, and the next morning all hands went aboard and started for Cahaba, at the time the Seat of Government.

At Cahaba, as in Montgomery, everything was "done up" as it should be. There the General met with Major Porter, whom he had known in the Revolution. There I shed more tears. The General examined the old ditch that had been cut by his countrymen many years before. An old cannon was shown him also, which was left by the French Army, when they quit the country. He remarked that those relics caused sad feelings, that there was still a pleasure, a kind of melancholy pleasure, which he could not describe.

About this time a gentleman was wounded from the firing a cannon on a trading boat. The General visited the wounded man, and took much interest in his welfare; he was told that the gentleman had many friends who would care for him; I told him that he was an old camp mate of mine; he replied, "one good soldier will always take care of another." I remained in Calaba until the General embarked on board, and on bidding him farewell, said: "I have done what little I could to make your journey to this place as pleasant as possible, and I now have to leave you." He took me by the hand and said: "I thank you kindly; may God bless and prosper the young and thriving State you live in; I shall always cherish the kindest feelings for you and the other gentlemen that escorted me through the nation, as well as all others who have taken so much trouble to make me welcome among you. The last words I heard him utter were, "Farewell, my friend! Take care of that wounded man."

XIV

WHEELING, WINN PARISH, LA.
AUGUST 12th, 1858

COL. ALBERT J. PICKETT

Dear Sir:

In my letter to you of 21st of June Last, which was published in *The Montgomery Mail* of the 23rd of July, I see a mistake that I will here correct. In speaking of Davy Tate, it is said he was not an educated man. Mr. Tate was an educated man; and if I am not mistaken, he informed me that he was educated near Abernethy, in Scotland, and was about ten years younger than Alexander McGuillivray. As I may at some time after this, speak more of Mr. Tate and his brother, Weatherford, I will leave them here....

I now say to you, without the fear of being contradicted by any one that knows, that Tallassees had never settled on the Tallapoosa river before 1756, they were moved to that place by James McQueen—McQueen settling himself at the same time near where Walter Lucas once had a stand, at the crossing of Line Creek; and it was at that place on Line Creek where the celebrated negro interpreter, John McQueen was

born. The Tallasses quit their old settlements in the Talladega country, and it was immediately occupied by a band of
Netches, under the control of a chief called Chenubby, and a
Hollander by the name of Moniac. This man was the father of
Sam Moniac, whom you in your history call McNae, thinking him to be of Scotch race. The chief Chennubby lived to
be a very old man. I knew him as well as I did any Indian in
the Nation. He was with Gen. Jackson in the Creek War; he
was with me in Florida in 1818. I have often by a camp fire sat
and listened to him tell over his troubles among the French,
on the Mississippi, and how the French had drove them from
their old homes; and how he had helped to drive the French
from their trading house at the forks of Coosa and Tallapoosa.
It was his son, young Chennubby, or Sarlotta Fixico, who left
Fort Leslie and went to Gen. Jackson's camp.

Yours,

T. S. W.

XV

WHEELING, WINN PARIS, LA.
SEPTEMBER 16, 1858

TO J. J. HOOKER, Esq.,

Dear Sir:
I do not take my pen in hand according to the old custom, but have it between my thumb and forefinger, and you can judge whether or not it improves my hieroglyphics. And as I have at times been detailing to you some few things about Indians and Indian customs, one thing I learned from them was that time was never an object with them, and at this time must follow their example—take my time.

I received a letter the other day from my worthy friend, the Knight of the Horse Shoe. I speak nothing but the truth when I say that I am truly glad to hear that he is still living and in good health. I hope he may live as long as suits his convenience. I don't know that I would care if he could live a thousand years, and die rich, so that I could be left to administer his estate.

I not long since received a letter purporting to be written by one George D. Taylor. I know it is not Col. George Taylor of Coosa, for he is my friend and a gentleman. If there be such a man as George D. Taylor, and he writes to me again, I will beg permission to answer him through your paper, and will pledge myself to give as true answer him through your paper, and will pledge myself to give as true a history of a person that he claims to be related to, as any one can give him that now lives.

Yours truly,

T. S. W.

XVI

WHEELING, WINN PARISH, LA.,
OCTOBER 20th, 1858

TO; J. J. HOOPER, Esq.,

Dear Sir,
Whenever a biographer, or one who writes sketches of the lives of others, no matter whether they be true or false, so long as he speaks in praise of the individual of whom he writes, he never can be charged with maliciously doing wrong, unless by chance or otherwise, he raises the reputation of his hero at the expense of another. But if an individual from the best of motives, undertakes to correct errors to set mankind right in relation to the true history of men and things, he is often charged with being influenced by, or from, malicious motives, or something worse; particularly should he write any thing that would be the least calculated to dim in a small degree the lustre thrown around some favorite by a good hearted, visionary biographer. But no truly conscientious man while living, could brook the idea of thanking a man, that after he was dead, would emblazon to the world a fame he was not entitled to, or ascribe to him deeds of daring that he had not

performed while living. For what I am now going to write, I will no doubt be censured by some. But what need I care, for I am now old, and it will not be long before I appear at a place where a life of truth will be worth more to me than all the good or bad opinions entertained of me by those I leave behind.

I have just been looking over Col. Pickett's sketches relative to Gen. Sam Dale. And I find them so utterly incorrect, and the history of the man (by Col. P.) so entirely different from what I know it to have been, or know it to be, I must at least be allowed to say, that the Colonel has a very fruitful imagination, or has been most egregiously imposed upon, or perhaps both.

But in justice to Col. Pickett, I must say, if I knew a man with little merit, that had seen one hostile Indian, a few teeth pulled, a few eyes and noses operated on, and a few fingers amputated, who wished his life written while living or after he was dead, and it praised according to the most approved style, by modern light readers, I would recommend him to the colonel, or the Colonel to him. For taking into consideration the subject of the Colonel's memoirs and the material he has had left him to work with, he can certainly color a picture as high as it will bear at least. I knew Gen. Dale before Col. P. was born, and knew him through life, and knew him well: none knew him better, and to give a true sketch of his life, would be to go back to Georgia and detail a hundred or more fist fights, and down to his last fight in Georgia, which was with John Wesley Webb, in Clinton, Jones county. Those who knew Gen. Dale will recollect the scars on his face; they were the flesh marks of John Wesley Webb.

Dale was an Indian trader, and traded with the Upper Towns in the Creek Nation, some of which I will name: the Ocfuskes, Cieligees, Fish Ponds or Tatloulgees, Hillabys, Netches, Talladegas, or the people of the border. His principal partner was Col. Harrison Young. The half-breed that Col. Pickett alludes to as his partner, was his interpreter, by the name of John Berfort or Berford, and partly raised by Gen. Adams. If Dale was ever a Colonel in the Georgia line and two Indians at Ocfuske, on the Cattahoochee, I never heard of it. There was a trading path that crossed the Chatahoochee going to Ocduske on the Tallapoosa, and a few Indians traded at it, but the only Ocfuske town in my time was at Tallapoosa. The Horse Shoe was called Ocfuske.

In point, I recollect Col. Fosh, he was once the Adjutant General of Georgia; the Georgians called him a Frenchman, but he was a Polander, and unfortunately for him and his men, the records giving an account of his exploits in Indian fighting have been lost. The only, or principal fight with whites and Creek Indians, between the Revolution and the War of 1813–14 that has been left on record, was Clark's fight at Jack's Creek; though there were some killed on both sides, before and after that. Not long after the fight with Webb, which I think was in 1810, Dale and Young moved to Mississippi Territory, near St. Stephens. It is a mistake about Dale being at the Indian Council at Tuckabatchy in 1811, at the time of Tecumseh's visit; and it is also a mistake about his having communicated to Col. Hawkins what was considered to be the object of Tecumseh's visit among the Creeks. For the Colonel had spies in the nation that watched the movements of him and the Big Warrior, and Billy McIntosh was one of them, and no white man was admitted into their councils; and could it now be ascertained to a certainty, I would hazard anything I have that Tecumseh, Seekaboo and their few followers were never seen by a half dozen white men that knew them, from the time they left the Wabash until they returned to the Warpicanatta Village. Christian Limbo, John Ward, Bob Walton and Nimrod Doyle saw Tecumseh at the Tallassee Square, opposite Tuckabatchy, and the reason why they were permitted to see him, was, that Walton and Doyle had known him in his younger days.

These men have described Tecumseh to me minutely, and what well satisfies me they did so, I lived neighbor to the late Col. Clever of Arkansas, who was Lieutenant in the last war, or war of 1812, and was at the battle of the Thames. It will be recollected by those who knew Col. Clever that he was a great friend of Col. Johnson, but denied him the credit of killing Tecumseh. He said Tecumseh was killed some time after Col. Johnson was wounded and disabled; that he was killed at least three hundr3ed yards from wher the Colonel was shot.

And while I am at it, I will go into minute detail of Col. Clever's statement, as it corroborates the statement made by Doyle and Walton. He said, from the way the Indians rallied and fought around a certain Indian until he was killed, and a small trinket found on his person, that he was supposed to be a chief. And there being but few if any among the whites that had known Tecumseh, except Gen. Harrison, it was some it was some time after the close of the fight before it was ascertained that the dead Chief was Tecumseh; and it was only ascertained through the General. The circumstance of the bold stand made by the supposed Chief being communicated to Gen. Harrison, he visited the spot where the dead Indian lay; the body was much mangled, and as the General approached the spot a soldier was in the act of taking off a piece of skin from the Indian's thigh. The General ordered the soldier to stop, said he regretted to know that he had such a man in his camp, and reprimanded him severely. He had some water brought, had the Indian washed and stretched his full-length, examined his teeth and pronounced it to be Tecumseh. One of Tecumseh's legs was a little smaller, and he had a halt in his walk that was perceptible, and he had a tooth, thought not decayed, of a bluish cast. This was Col. Clever's statement, that I have heard him make a hundred times and his description corroborates that of Doyle and Walton, of Tecumseh. At all events, Tecumseh was killed at the battle of the Thames; history, or some portion of it, gives the credit to Col. Johnson; I have given Col. Clever's account of that affair, without giving my opinion as to who killed him. And there is but one man that I know of living that could give any satisfactory evidence of that matter—it is Gen. Lefis Cass, the present Secretary of State, of the United States.

I will now go back to where I am better acquainted. Gen. Dale was in the Burnt Corn battle, but from what I have learned from the late Judge Lipscomb, of Texas, formerly of Alabama, and others, on the part of the whites, and Jim Boy, the principal War Chief, that was with McQueen, and whom. P. styles "High Head Jim," the whole affair was but a light one. The Canoe Fight was reality—I knew all the party, that is, Gen. Dale, Col. Austill, James Smith and the negro Caesar. Col. Austill is yet living, and of course knows more of the fight than I could possibly know. But I have no doubt that he will say that the fight has been detailed by Col. Pickett to the best advantage of those engaged in it; and will also say that an Indian fight, either in a canoe or the bushes alters its appearance very much by getting into a book or newspaper. I have heard the accounts given, from Gen. Dale down to Caesar; it's a pity the eight big Indians killed in the canoe had not been taken to the shore for the landsmen to have looked at.

Col. Pickett says a few years before that, that Gen. Dale was in the act of drinking, when two Indians tried to tomahawk him; that he knifed them, took their trail carrying five bleeding wounds, brained three more warriors, released a female prisoner and she killed a fourth. That's another exploit I never heard of. I suspect the woman's dead by now; and whether this startling event was in the Georgia wars between the Revolution and the war of 1813–14, or at what period or place, we are not told. The account only says some years before the Canoe fight.

I could not help smiling when I read the Colonel's account of the Roman Consul, Acquilius, and comparing a case of Gen. Dale's in Mobile to that of the Consul's. Silence, I think, would have been the strongest appeal that persons in their situations could have made, particularly in Mobile, and would have evinced more greatness in both the General and Consul.

Now, sir, let me tell you who General Dale was and what he was: he was honest, he was brave, he was kind to a fault, his mind was of the ordinary kind, not well cultivated, fond of speculation and not well fitted for it; a bad manager in money matters and often embarrassed, complained much of others for his misfortunes, was very combative, always ready to go into danger; would hazard much for a friend and was charitable in pecuniary matters, even to those he looked upon as enemies. I could relate many little frolics of his that might be interesting to a few, but as such things are witnessed almost daily, particularly where whiskey is drunk, I shall not mention them. He spent much of his time with me in 1834. He knew very little about Indian character, and entertained a good feeling for that persecuted people. So soon as he had an enemy in his power he was done, and would sympathize with and for him, and at times would cry like a child. I have given you the true character of Gen. Dale, and those that were old enough and were intimately acquainted with him, will tell you I have given a faithful account of the man as far as I have gone. What I have written is to correct error, not to detract, and you never can take from a man that which he never had. What Col. Pickett has written of Gen. Dale and others that I know, would do for a novel, but not history. Men who write history and wish to deal a little in the marvelous for the amusement of readers, should look around and see who is living, particularly if they are writing about things that have happened in their own time, and a little before.

I will, in a day or two, write out and send you the true character of Billy Weatherford and the part he acted in the war—some things I personally know, and others I obtained from Weatherford himself, and he was truly what the Indians called him. Billy Larney, or Yellow Billy, was one of his names; his other was Hoponicafutsahia, or Truth Maker or Teller. And as Col. Pickett has failed to give us a history of the war of 1836–7, in Alabama, and as I participated with him and others in that memorable struggle to see who could get first into Mr. Belser's paper, and for fear some may die off and not do it, I will write that out and send it to you.

It will be seen that I have alluded to Col. Johnson, and that there are doubts as to his killing Tecumseh; it matters not who killed Tecumseh; Col. Johnson proved himself a distinguished man, not only as a soldier, but in everything else that he has undertaken. And that is a subject I should not have alluded to here, but I see in Col. Pickett's history that he says Gen. Dale saw Tecumseh at the council with the Creek Indians in 1811, which I am certain is incorrect. Persons that have not read Col. Pickett's *History of Alabama*, will lose much of my meaning. And notwithstanding many of the Colonel's pictures are highly wrought and his information and his knowledge of the modern Creeks and their war with the whites in 1813–14, are very imperfect, his history is very well written, and will be found by those who have not read it an interesting work. I will close this by simply remarking that it matters not whose reputation history raises, or whose character it damages, it is the duty of all that can do so, to correct its errors.

Respectfully,

T. S. W.

XVII

WHEELING, WINN PARISH, LA.,
OCTOBER 31st, 1858

TO J. J. HOOPER, Esq.

Dear Sir:

Some months back I addressed a letter to Mr. Rutherford at Union springs, containing some of the incidents of the life of Billy Weatherford. Not having seen it published, I have concluded to give you a few sketches of the history of that man and the part he took in the war of 1813–14. His father was Charles Weatherford, a white man, that came to the Creek Nation shortly after the close of the American Revolution, in company with Sam Mims, who was once engaged with George Galpin in the Indian trade. Weatherford's mother was half breed Tuskegee; her father was a Scotchman by the name of Malcolm McPherson, and a blood relation to the late Judge Berrien, of Georgia. Schoy, or Sehoya McPherson was brought up in her early days by the father of Sam Moniac. She lived a part of her time with Lauchlan McGillivray and Daniel McDonald. Her first husband was Col. John Tate, the last agent the English had among the Creeks. By Tate she had one son, Davy, who is remembered by many who are yet living. Davy Tate was a man of fine sense, great firmness and very kind to those with whom he was intimate, and remarkably charitable to strangers. But circumstances caused Tate to mix but little with the world after the country fell into the hands of the whites and he never was well known by but few after that.

I have stated to you before that Col. Tate died deranged between Flint River and Chattahoochee, and was buried near old Cuseta. Charles Weatherford was the second and last husband of Sehoy McPherson. They raised four children that I knew. Betsy, the oldest child, married Sam Moniac, and was the mother of Major David Moniac, who was educated at West Point and was killed by the Seminoles in the fall of 1836—he was educated at West Point in consequence of the faithful and disinterested friendship of his father to the whites. Billy was the next oldest, Jack next, and a younger daughter whose name I have forgotten. She married Capt. Shumac, a very intelligent officer of the United States army.

I had seen Billy Weatheford before the war, but only knew him from character. The circumstance of him and Moniac aiding Col. Hawkins in the arrest of Bowles, made them generally known to the people of Georgia who wished to know anything about Indians. It would be too tedious to tell how I first became acquainted with Weatherford. I was with Gen. Floyd in the Nation, and was at his night fight at Calebee; a few days after the fight the army returned to fort Hull. The time was about expiring for which the troops had to serve, and a call was made for volunteers to take charge of the fort until the Militia from the two Carolinas could arrive. Cap. John H. Broadnax, a very efficient and popular captain, from Putnam county, Georgia, soon raised a company of infantry; a Lieutenant Adaroin from Franklin county raised a rifle corps, and I volunteered as his Orderly Sergeant. A few days before that, the present Gen. Twiggs, than a Captain in the regular army, had forced his way through to the army with his company. The army left, and the three companies above mentioned took charge of the Fort, Col. Homer V. Milton in command.

All I recollect to have done myself was to take some authority that one of my rank was not entitled to, under the rules and articles of war, and Capt. Twiggs put me in stocks. And for fear you may thing the case worse than it was, I will say to you that I only rendered another Sergeant unfit for duty. I think the whole story would amuse you if you could hear it, but it would be too long for the present; I may give it to you hereafter. I was in the stocks but a few minutes before I was released, and I think that after that I was rather a favorite both with the Captain and the Colonel.

The Colonel wanted an express sent to Gen. Graham at Fort Mitchell. It had to be taken on foot; I volunteered my services, and got George Lovittt, a tall half breed; and obtained a pair of shoes from an Irishman by the name of James Gorman, whom I had known near two years before that in Florida, in the Spanish Patriot service, under my old and intimate friend, Billy Cone. The distance was only forty-five miles. Lovitt and I went in one night, got everything ready and returned to Fort Hull the next night. The troops began to arrive at the Fort, and the Militia under Capt. Broadnax and Lieut. Adaroin, were permitted to leave for home. Col. Milton employed me to go to Fort Hawkins and bring a horse and some baggage left with Col. Cook, which I did. On my return, I found the Colonel at Fort Decatur. On the receipt of his horse and baggage, he gave me a very substantial Indian pony, and proposed to me to remain with him until he reached his regiment, the old 3d Infantry, then at Alabama Heights, under the command of Lieut. Col. Russell, and that he could procure me the appointment of Lieutenant in the army, to be attached to his regiment. I was not ambitious of military honors, and concluded to join the Indians.

I had been paid for my services in the previous campaign, had a pony, and that was all I needed. I made up a mess with Sam Sells, John Winslet, Billy McIntosh, Joe Marshall, Sam Moniac and others, and went where it suited me. This gave me an opportunity of becoming acquainted with all the little hostile bands and their leaders. As I have described to you before how the most of them were situated after Gen. Jackson reached the fork of the two rivers, Coosa and Tallapoosa, it will not be necessary now to do so.

Though Weatherford was still at Moniac's Island when I reached Gen. Jackson's camp, Tom Carr, or Tuskegeee Emarthla, came up and learned through Moniac that Billy Weatherford could come in with safety, as Col. Hawkins had taken it upon himself to let the General know who and what he, Weatherford, was. I one day went out with Sucky Cornells and others to Cornells' old cow pens to see Jim Boy and Paddy Welch, who had been one of the principal leaders in the fight against Gen. Floyd. Welch was afterward hanged near Clairborne, for killing a man by the name of Johnson and another by the name of McCaskill or McCorkell.

Jim Boy's camp was not far from Pole Cat Springs, on the Cubahatchy, and near where he built a little town after that which was called Thlopthlocco. On our return to camp, Weatherford, Tom Carr, Otis Harjo, Catsa Harjo or Mad Tiger, a Coowersartda Chief, and a host of others had come in, so I missed hearing the great speech or seeing Ben Baldwin's white horse or the deer. The horse I never heard of, nor him, until I found him in Col. Pickett's history of Alabama.

There was a talk with the General and Weatherford and some Chiefs, and of course I did not hear it as I was not permitted to be at headquarters at that day, being looked upon as another Indian. But I think I know the purport of the talk as well as any one living or dead, for I knew both the men well, long after that, and have hear both of them talk it over; and I will give you, as near as I can, what I understood passed at their first interview. Gen. Jackson said to Weatherford, that he was astonished a man of his good sense, and almost a white man, to take sides with an ignorant set of savages, and being led astray by men who professed to be prophets and gifted with a supernatural influence. And more than all, he had led the Indians and was one of the prime movers of the massacre at Fort Mims.

Weatherford listened attentively to the General until he was through. He then said to the General, that much had been charged to him that he was innocent of, and that he believed as little in Indian or white prophets as any man living, and that he regretted the unfortunate destruction of Fort Mims and its inmates as much as he, the General, or any one else. He said it was true he was at Fort Mims when the attack was made, and it was but a little while after the attack was made before the hostile Indians seemed inclined to abandon their undertaking; that those in the Fort, and particularly the half breeds under Dixon Bailey, poured such a deadly fire into their ranks as caused them to back out for a short time; at this stage of the fight he, Weatherford, advised them to draw off entirely. He then left to go some few miles to where his half brother, Davy Tate, had some negroes, to take charge of them, to keep the Indians from scattering them; after he left, the Indians succeeded in firing the Fort, and waited until it burnt so that they could enter it with but little danger. He also said to the General that if he had joined the whites it would have been attributed to cowardice and not thanked. And moreover, it was his object in joining the Indians, that he thought he would in many instances be able to prevent them from committing depredations upon defenseless persons; and but for the mismanagement of those that had charge of the Fort, he would have succeeded, and said, "Now, sir, I have told the truth, if you think I deserve death, do as you please; I shall only beg for the protection of a starving parcel of women and children, and those ignorant men who have been led into the war by their Chiefs."

This is as much as I ever learned from the General, and I will proceed to give Weatherford's own statement, which I have often heard him make. But before I go further, I will here remark, why I think the story of the white horse and deer have been played off on the credulity of Col. Pickett, as well as other things I see in his history that I know of my own knowledge, and so do others, to be incorrect. After it was known that Gen. Jackson would punish any one that was known to trouble an Indian coming to camp unarmed, and particularly Weatherford, the Indians were put to searching the country for something to eat, particularly those who had been lying out. Moniac was under the impression that he could find some cattle in the neighborhood of his cowpens, on the Pinchong creek. Several Indian countrymen and myself went with the Indians in search of the cattle. Weatherford went with the crowd, and had to get a horse from Barney Riley, having none of his own; besides, had the exhibition of the white horse and deer been a reality, Major Eaton and others who made speeches for Weatherford would certainly have noticed it. It has been many years since I read what purported to be Weatherford's speech when he surrendered to Gen. Jackson; but if I recollect right, he was made to say that he would whip the Georgians on one side of the river and make his corn on the other. That was all a lie, and for effect.

I will go back to our cow hunt. At Moniac's cowpens we found no cattle, but killed plenty of deer and turkeys, and picked up the half brother of Jim Boy—George Goodwin.

Now let us turn to Weatherford. He was a man of fine

sense, great courage, and knew much about out government and mankind in general—had lived with his half-brother Davy Tate, who was an educated and well-informed man—had been much with his brother-in-law, Sam Moniac, who was always looked upon as being one of the most intelligent half-breeds in the Nation, and was selected by Alexander Mc-Gillivray for interpreter at the time he visited Gen. Washington in New York. Although it has been said that McGillivray mastered the Latin and Greek languages, and although the letters of Alexander Leslie are published to the world as Mc-Gillivray's productions, he (McG.) knew too well how matters stood, and relied on Moniac. I have often seen a medal that Gen. Washington gave Moniac. He always kept it on his person, and it is with him in his grave at Pass Christian.

Some time in April 1814, on the West bank of the Pinchong, now in Montgomery county, Ala., and by a camp fire, I heard Weatherford relate the following particulars about the creek war:

He said that some years before the war, a white man came from Pensacola to Tuckabatchy. He remained some time with the Big Warrior. The white man was a European, and he thought a Scotchman; that he never knew the man's business, nor did he ever learn; that all the talks between this man and the Big Warrior were carried on through a negro interpreter that belonged to the Warrior; that he (Weatherford) had seen the man several times, and more than once the man asked how many warriors he thought the Creeks could raise. The man disappeared from the Nation, and in a short time Tuskenea, the oldest son of the Big Warrior, took a trip to the Wabash, and visited several tribes—the Shawnees or Sowanakas.

(This trip Tuskenea did make, for I have often heard him speak of it, and have seen some women of the Hopungiesas and Shawnees that he carried to the Creek Nation.) Weatherford said that not long after the return of Tuskenea to the creek Nation, Tecumseh, with the Prophet, Seekaboo, and others made their appearance at the Tuckabatchy town. A talk was put out by the Warrior. Moniac and Weatherford attended the talk. No white man was allowed to be present. Tecumseh stated the object of his mission; that if it could be effected, the Creeks could recover all the country that the white had taken from them, and the British would protect them in their right. Moniac was the first to oppose Tecumseh's talk, and said that the talk was a bad one, and that he (Tecumseh) had better leave the Nation. The Big Warrior seemed inclined to take the talk. The correspondence was carried on through Seekaboo, who spoke English.

After Moniac had closed, Weatherford then said to Seekaboo to say to Tecumseh, that the whites and Indians were doing well, and that it would be bad policy for the creeks, at least, to take sides either with the Americans or English, in the event of a war (that was in 1811.) Besides, he said, that when the English held sway over the country, they were equally as oppressive as the Americans had been, if not more so; and in the American revolution the Americans were but few, and that they had got the better of the English; and that they were now very strong, and if interest was to be consulted, the Indians had better join the Americans.

After this talk Tecumseh left for home, and prevailed on Seekaboo and one or two others to remain among the Creeks.

In 1812 the Indians killed Arthur Lott and Thomas Meridith, which I before mentioned, as well as Captain Isaacs' going to the mouth of Duck river. After this, matters calmed down until the opening of 1813. Moniac and Weatherford took a trip to the Chickasawha in Mississippi Territory, trading in beef cattle. On their return, they found that several chiefs had assembled at a place that was afterwards settled by one Townsend Robinson, from Anson county, N.C. They were taking the Ussa, or black drink, and had Moniac's and Weatherford's families at the square. They told Moniac and Weatherford that they should join or be put to death. Moniac boldly refused, and mounted his horse. Josiah Francis, his brother-in-law seized his bridle. Moniac snatched a war club from his hand, gave him a severe blow and put out, with a shower of rifle bullets following him. Weatherford consented to remain. He told them that he disapproved their course, and that it would be their ruin; but they were his people; he was raised with them, and he would share their fate. He was no chief, but had much influence with the Indians. He was always called by the Indians Billy Larney, or Yellow Billy; that was his boy name. His other name was Hoponika Futsahia. Hoponika Futsahia, as near as I can give the English of it, is Truthmaker—and he was all of that.

He then proposed to the Indians to collect up all such as intended going to war with the whites; take their women and children into the swamps of Florida; leave the old men and lads to hunt for them, and the picked warriors to collect together and operate whoever it was thought best. He said he had several reasons for making this proposition to the Alabama river Indians; one was, that he thought by the time they could take their women and children to Florida and return, that the upper Creek towns, which were almost to a man hostile, except the Netches and Hillabys—and were principally controlled by the Ocfuske chief, Menauway, or Ogillis Ineha, or Fat Englishman (these were the names of the noted men who headed the Indians at Horse Shoe);—that they would perhaps come to terms, and by that means his people would be spared and not so badly broken up, and would be the means of saving the lives of many whites on the thinly settled frontiers; and if the worst came to the worst, that they could carry on the war with less trouble, less danger, and less expense, than to be troubled with their woman and children.

But in all this he was overruled by the chiefs. Some of their names I will give you. The oldest and principal chief, the one looked upon as the General, was a Tuskegee, called Hopie Tustanugga, or Far-off-Warrior; he was killed at Fort Mims. The others were Peter McQueen, Jim Boy, or High-head Jim. Illes Harjo, or Josiah Francis, the new made Prophet, the Otisee chief Nehemarthla-Micco, Paddy Welch, Hossa Yohola, and Seekaboo, the Shawnee prophet, and many others I could name.

The first thing to be had was ammunition. Peter McQueen, with Jim Boy as his war chief, with a party of Indians, started for Pensacola. (Their numbers have been greatly overrated.) On their route, at Burnt Corn Springs, they took Betsy Coulter, the wife of Jim Cornells (not Alexander Cornells, who was the Government interpreter); they carried her to Pensacola, and sold her to a French lady, a madame Barrone. At Pensacola they met up with Zach McGirth, and some of them wanted to kill him. Jim Boy interfered, and said the man or men who harmed McGirth should die.

Now, recollect, I lived with these people long, and have heard these things over and over. Betsy Coulter lived with me for years, as well as others, who bore their parts on one side or the other. This is history—it is as true as Gospel—for I am now and was then a living witness to much of it, and have seen the others who witnessed the balance—and the witnesses to the other have been dead a long time; and besides, what I have seen and write is nothing more than what is and has been common.

But on the return of McQueens' party from Pensacola, the fight took place at Burnt Corn creek between the Indians and at least three times their number of white men; that is, if we take the statements of the two commanders, Col. Collier and Jim Boy. Jim Boy said the war had not fairly broke out, and that they never thought of being attacked; that he did not start with a hundred men, and all of those he did start with were not in the fight. I have heard Jim tell it often, that if the whites had not stopped to gather up pack horses and plunder their camp, and had pursued the Indians a little further, they (the Indians) would have quit and gone off. But the Indians discovered the very great disorder the whites were in, searching for plunder, and they fired a few guns from the creek swamp and a general stampede was the result. McGirth always corroborated Jim Boy's statement as to the number of Indians in the Burnt Corn fight. I have seen many of those who were in the fight, and they were like the militia that were at Bladensburg—-they died off soon; you could never hear much talk about the battle, unless you met with such a man as Judge Lipscomb, who used to make a laughing matter of it.

Enough of the Burnt Corn battle now. A part of the Indians returned to Pensacola, and some went to the Nation. So soon as those who had gone back the second time to Pensacola returned, they commenced fitting out an expedition to Fort Mims. Weatherford said that he delayed them as much as possible on their march, in order that those in the fort might be prepared. They took several negroes on the route, and it was made convenient to let them escape; that he had understood that an office with some troops had reached Fort Mims, and had quite a strong force, but had no expectation of taking it whatever, until the morning they got within view of the Fort; that he was close enough to the Fort to recognize Jim Cornells—saw him as he rode up to the Fort and rode off. I have seen Cornells often since and heard him tell it; he rode to the Fort and told Maj. Beasley that he has seen some Indians, and the Fort would be attacked that day.

Maj. Beasley was drunk; he said to Cornells that he had only seen a gang of red cattle. Cornells told the Major that that gang of red cattle would give him a hell of a kick before night. As Cornells rode off Zach McGirth followed him out, and went to the boat yard; they were to provision a boat up, and while McGirth was out the boat was attacked; that is the way he escaped. The Fort gate was open and could not be shut, and a number of the Indians followed a Shawnee (not Seekaboo) who pretended to be a Prophet; he was leathered from top to toe. Dixon Bailey ran up within a few yards of him and placed the Prophet where even the Witch of Endor could not reach him. Some of the Prophet's followers being served in the same way, the rest left the Fort. This I learned from McGirth, Sam Smith and others who were saved and escaped from the Fort, as well as from Jim Boy, Weatherford and others who were engaged in the assault.

The Indians then pretty well ceased operations, and Weatherford, as I have remarked before, left and went off to take charge of his brother's negroes. After he left, the Shawnee, Seekaboo, and some of the McGillivray negroes got behind some logs that were near the Fort, kindled a fire, and, by putting rags on their arrows and setting them on fire, would shoot them into the roof of Mims' smokehouse, which was an old building, and formed a part of one line of the Fort. It took fire and communicated it to the other buildings—and that is the way Fort Mims was destroyed.

Jim Boy succeeded in saving Mrs. Girth and her daughter, but her only son, James, was killed. Weatherford's taking charge of Tate's negroes gave rise to the report by some whites that there was an understanding between him and Tate that one was to remain with the whites, and the other with the Indians. The report was, no doubt, false, but it ever after caused Tate to be very reserved with most people. I knew Tate well. He, like Weatherford, was an honest man; but many have done him great injustice.

After the Fort fell, and Jim Boy saved Mrs. McGirth and tried to save others, the Indians ran him off, and it was sometime before they would be reconciled to him. After plundering the Fort, they scattered in various directions and made their way back to the Nation, except a few.

The Indians expected after this that the whites would pour into the Nation from all quarters, and most of them that were at Fort Mims returned to where Robinson had a plantation afterwards, and the place that Moniac had escaped from. The reason why they selected that place was, that there was on the North side of the river Nocoshatchy, or Bear creek, that which afforded the most impenetrable swamps in the whole country. But the movements of the whites were so slow that the Indians grew careless, and a few Indians, with Weatherford and the chief, Hossa Yoholo, and one or two others, made what has been known as the Holy Ground their head-quarters. Some time in December, Gen. Claiborne, piloted by Sam Moniac and an old McGillivray negro, got near the place before the Indians discovered them. The Indians began to cross their wives and children over the river; they had scarcely time to do that before the army arrived—a skirmish ensued, and the Indians, losing a few men, gave way in every direction. Weatherford was among the last to quit the place. He made an attempt to go down the river—that is, down the bank of the river—but found that the soldiers would intercept his passage, and he turned up, keeping on the bluff near the river, until he reached the ravine or little branch that makes into the river above where the town used to be. There was a small foot-path that crossed the ravine near the river; he carried his horse down that path, and instead of going out of the ravine at the usual crossing, he kept up it towards its head, until he passed the lines of the whites. So, now, you have the fluff-jumping story.

This story was told long before Weatherford died. Maj. Cowles and myself asked him how that report got out. He said Sam Moniac knew him, and seeing him on horseback on the brink of the bluff, and his disappearing so suddenly, caused those who saw him to believe that he had gone over the bluff. He said that he ran a greater risk in going the way he did, than he would to have gone over it and crossed the river. But it was to save his pony that he risked passing between two lines of the whites. From that circumstance the report got out, and he would often own to it for the gratification of some, as they wanted to be deceived anyhow. But in going the way he did, it was hazarding more than one in a thousand would do, for a hundred times the value of a pony.

There was one Indian, if no more, killed at Holy Ground. I believe it from this circumstance. Some years after the fight, and the whites began to settle Alabama, a very poor man by the name of Stoker settled on the Autauga side, and opposite Holy Ground. His little boys, while out hunting one day, found the irons of an old trunk and some $100 or $200 in eagle half dollars; this I have no doubt, was plundered at Fort Mims, and the plunderer placed it where the boys of Stoker found it, and went back into the fight at Holy Ground and was killed.

Weatherford said that after he escaped from the Holy Ground, he began to think over what was next to be done; the Indians were without ammunition, but little to eat, armies marching in from all quarters; the Spaniards at Pensacola seemed afraid to aid them, as they had done at the commencement—everything seemed to forbode the destruction of him and his people. He fell in with Savannah or Sowanoka Jack, and they consulted together as to what was best. Jack proposed to get as many of their people as they could; that in a few years the whites would entirely surround them; the Spaniards in Florida would afford them no protection. They then agreed to watch the movements of the Georgia army, to see if there could be no chance to get ammunition. They did so; and waited until Gen. Floyd camped near Calebee. They had collected the largest number of warriors that had been collected during the war. They saw that Gen. Floyd intended crossing the creek, from his quitting the Tuckabatchy route.

The night before the fight, which commenced before day, the Indians camped near what was called McGarth's still house branch, on the west side of the branch, and held a council. He (Weatherford) proposed to wait until the army started to cross the creek, and as the advanced guard reached the hill on the next side, the fire on the guard should be the signal for the attack; that the army was small, a chance to get hold of the ammunition, if they did not defeat the whites. But to attack the whites in their camp, who were well supplied with ammunition and five pieces of cannon, would be folly, unless the Indians had more ammunition. The chiefs overruled him, and he, with a few Tuskegees, quit the camp and started back, and when he reached Pole Cat Springs he heard the firing commence. It is my belief that had Weatherford's advice been taken, the result of that affair would have been very different; for long before the fight closed, I could understand Indian enough to hear them asking each other to "give me some bullets—give me powder." The friendly Indians with us did us no good, except Timpoochy Barnard and his Uchees. Jim Boy and Billy McDonald, or Billy McGillivray, as he was best known, said that they had between 1800 and 2000 men; but many of them were without guns, and only had war-clubs and bow and arrows.

The surrender of Weatherford to Gen. Jackson you have had from various sources—you must judge who you think most correct. I have heard Gen. Jackson say that if he was capable of forming anything like a correct judgment of a man on a short acquaintance, that he pronounced Weatherford to be as high-toned and fearless as any man he had met with—one whose very nature scorned a mean action. And Gen. Jackson's treatment to Billy Weatherford proved that he believed what he said; for, had Weatherford proved any other than Jackson took him to be, he would have met the fate of Francis and Nehemarthla-Micco.

What I have here written is as correct as my memory will allow, for I have no history to refer to.

XVIII

WHEELING, WINN PARISH, LA.
NOVEMBER 3, 1858

J. J. HOOPER Esq.,

Dear Sir:
A day or two since I sent you some sketches of the life of Billy
Weatherford, in which I forgot to say that he never was in
the hearing of the fire of a gun during the Creek war, except
at Fort Mims, Holy Ground, and Floyd's battle at Calebee
Creek, and only heard the firing at Calebee from Pole Cat
Springs.

In a letter addressed to me through the *Mail*, by Col. Pickett, in February last, he says that himself and I are as well
acquainted with the modern Creek Indians, perhaps, as any
two persons living. That may be so; but I think there is this
difference between us: his information has been derived from
very vague testimony, and gathered up at too late a date to
form anything like a true or correct history; and unfortunately
for me, too much of mine has been from personal experience
and from the most authentic testimony, and at an early day.
It is true that one so capable of writing as the Colonel could

have given the world not only a tolerably true, but quite an interesting history.

James McQueen was the first white man I ever heard of being among the Creeks. He was born in 1683—went into the Nation in 1716, and died in 1811. He married a Tallassee woman. The Tallassees then occupied a portion of Talladega county. In 1756 he moved the Tallassees down opposite Tuckabatchy, and settled the Netches under the chief Chenubby and Dixon Moniac, a Hollander, who was the father of Sam Moniac, at the Tallassee old fields, on the Tallasahatchy creek. McQueen settled himself on Line creek, in Montgomery county. I knew several of his children—that is, his sons, Bob, Fullunny and Peter. Bob was a very old man when I first knew him. He and Fullunny had Indian wives. Peter, the youngest son married Betsy Durant. They raised one son, James, and three daughters. Milly, Nancy and Tallassee. The Big Warrior's son, Yargee, had the three sisters for wives at the same time, and would have taken more half sisters. After Peter McQueen died, his widow returned from Florida and married Willy McQueen, the nephew of Peter and raised two daughters, Sophia and Muscogee, and some two or three boys. Old James McQueen had a daughter named Ann, commonly called Nancy. He called her after the queen of England, whose service he quit when he came into the Nation. Of late years it was hard to find a young Tallassee without some of the McQueen blood in his veins.

XIX

WHEELING, WINN PARISH, LA.
November 27, 1858

TO: J. J. HOOPER, Esq.,

Dear Sir:
My health has been bad of late—so much so, that I have been unable to write. I sent you a few days back a little document containing some corrections of errors in my printed letters. You will find that in the hand-writing of my son, Thomas, and I believe without date.

You will discover from what I have written, that I differ from Col. A. J. Pickett in some things relative to the early history of Alabama, and more particularly that of the Creek Indians. Notwithstanding I have differed from him as to history, I agree with all who knew him, that he was a high-toned gentleman, and his loss is much to be lamented. Col. Pickett possessed to a great degree a trait that is seldom, if ever, possessed by any but the best of man—that is, too great a confidence in the honesty of mankind. That doubt has been the cause of some things appearing in his history which a few of us old ones know to be incorrect. He has lived to inform himself, and to instruct his fellow man, and never (as I have heard) engaged in the political broils and troubles that have agitated the country in his time. That of itself is enough to make his memory revered by all who knew him.

He (Governor Bagby) was a man of fine sense and good heart. It was often said of him, that he was a bad manager in money matters, and did not accumulate wealth. But he could have done so, no doubt, had he wished it at any time; thought like a man of sense, he chose to live well on what he made, and never, like many others, cared to have large sums lying by him, merely to hear fools say that he had it.

Now for my friend, Col. Charles McLemore. The *Chambers Tribune* speaks nothing but the truth, when it says, "he was no ordinary man"; and if Chamber has not been left an orphan, the orphan's friend has left Chambers. I knew him when he was a little boy; his father died when he (Charles) was very young, leaving him and another, Frank, to make their way through the world as best they could.

Charles McLemore was most emphatically what the world terms a self-made man. He was endowed by nature with a fine intellect, and with that great share of moral honesty which has marked all his family whom I have known (and I have known many of them). He raised himself to what you have seen and know of him. I am unable to say any thing that could raise Charley McLemore any higher in the estimation of those who knew him, than the position he occupied at his death. When I left Georgia, and made Alabama my home, Charley was a little boy; I think he then lived in Jones county. Some twelve years afterwards, I met an intelligent young man at an Indian Council aat Oweatumpka-chee, or Falls of Little Uchee Creek (where my old friend and camp-mate, Col. Henry Moffett, afterwards erected some mills). This young man was Charles McLemore. I there renewed my acquaintance with him. What I am now going to relate will be remembered by many now living. The Council was in

the fall of 1832. Some Cherokees had been invited or requested by the whites to attend the Council, in order to encourage the Creeks to emigrate. Among the Cherokees were old Ridge, and his son, John Ridge (who has been killed since by the Ross family in Arkansas), Davy Van, and others. The Creeks were soured, and I knew it—for I lived within two miles of the head chief and knew his feelings, and communicated them to Col. Crowell. He soon discovered the great disinclination the chiefs had to going into Council, and used every exertion to prevent liquor being brought into camp. But by some means, some negroes belonging to a half breed, Joe Marshall, got some whiskey into camp. There was an order of it to be destroyed, and the whiskey was poured out on the ground, which seemed not to suit the tastes of some whites as well as Indians. It appeared that a white man had hired the negroes to carry the whiskey to camp, and it was proposed to flog the negroes; but Marshall objected, stating that the white men were to blame. A general fight commenced with the Indians themselves, and a great many whites left the camp, not knowing but that a general massacre was to take place. Marshall's party was the weakest, and seemed to be giving way. I remarked to McLemore, who was standing by me, that Marshall was a good man, and had been a great friend to the whites in the Creek war, and that I disliked to see him backed out; that was enough—Charley walked into the thickest of it, among the knives, clubs, and everything else. Wherever he went he opened their ranks, and Marshall soon quit winner. That was Charles McLemore. I have seen some trouble, and think I know something of men; but there is not one in a hundred who would have risked so much and showed the daring that McLemore did that night, and under such circumstances. Peace to the good and brave.

Yours, &c.,

T. S. W.

LaVergne, TN USA
15 March 2011
220053LV00001B/18/P